Library of
Davidson College

Legal Almanac Series No. 64

THE LAW OF SELF-DEFENSE:
Legal and Ethical Principles

by IRVING J. SLOAN

Irving J. Sloan
General Editor

1987
Oceana Publications, Inc.
London • Rome • New York

This is the sixty-fourth number in a series of LEGAL ALMANACS which bring you the law on various subjects in nontechnical language. These books do not take the place of your attorney's advice, but they can introduce you to your legal rights and responsibilities.

345.73
B347L
1987

87-5719

Library of Congress Catalog Card Number: 86-063541
ISBN: 0-379-11157-8

© Copyright 1987 by Oceana Publications, Inc.

All rights reserved. No part of this publication may be reproduced or transmitted in any form or by any means, electronic or mechanical, including photocopy, recording, xerography, or any information storage and retrieval system, without permission in writing from the publisher.

Manufactured in the United States of America

TABLE OF CONTENTS

Chapter 1
THE COMMON LAW: JUSTIFIABLE AND
 EXCUSABLE HOMICIDE THEORY 1

Chapter 2
THE PRINCIPLES OF SELF-DEFENSE IN
 OUTLINE 7

Chapter 3
THE AGGRESSOR'S RIGHT TO SELF-
 DEFENSE 13

Chapter 4
THE ISSUE OF RETREAT 17

Chapter 5
THE CONCEPT OF "FORCE" IN SELF-
 DEFENSE 23

Chapter 6
THE BATTERED WIFE SYNDROME AND
 THE IMPERFECT RIGHT TO SELF-
 DEFENSE 29

Chapter 7
THE BERNHARD GOETZ CASE 35

Chapter 8
SELF-DEFENSE IN INTERNATIONAL LAW 41

Epilogue
THE RIGHT OF SELF-DEFENSE: A
 QUESTION OF VALUES AND LAW 49

Appendices
  A. SELECTED STATE STATUTE
     PROVISIONS ON SELF-DEFENSE 55

  B. AMERICAN LAW INSTITUTE
     MODEL PENAL CODE 97

- C. AMERICAN LAW INSTITUTE MODEL PENAL CODE COMMENTS 101
- D. SELECTED EXCERPTS FROM OPINIONS ON SELF-DEFENSE 105
- E. LEADING CLASSICAL U.S. SUPREME COURT DECISIONS ON THE LAW OF SELF-DEFENSE 117
- F. SELF-DEFENSE PLEA AT NÜRNBERG 145

Index 147

. . . There does exist . . ., gentlemen, a law which is a law not of the statute-book, but the nature; a law which we possess not by instruction, tradition, or reading, but which we have caught, imbibed, and sucked in at Nature's own breast; a law which comes to us not by education but by constitution, not by training but by intuition—the law, I mean, that, should our life have fallen into any snare, into the violence and the weapons of robbers or foes, every method of winning a way to safety, would be morally justifiable. When arms speak, the laws are silent; they bid none to await their word, since he who chooses to await it must pay an undeserved penalty ere he can exact a deserved one.

Cicero, *Pro T. Annio Milone* (On Behalf of Milo) in The Speeches (N.H. Watts, trans.) 17 (1931). The speech was prepared in 52 B.C.

Chapter 1

THE COMMON LAW: JUSTIFIABLE AND EXCUSABLE HOMICIDE THEORY

At common law, homicide committed in self-defense is either justified or excusable.

Justifiable self-defense is where a person who is without fault himself is *feloniously* assaulted, necessarily kills his assailant to save himself from death or *great bodily harm,* or from some other felony attempted by force or surprise.

The conditions under which a homicide is justifiable on the ground of self-defense are:

1. Reasonably apparent imminent danger of death, or of some other felony, or of great bodily harm.
2. Danger need not necessarily be real, but it must be believed on reasonable grounds to be real.

Excusable self-defense is where a person becomes engaged in a sudden affray or combat, and in the course of the affray or combat necessarily, or under reasonably apparent necessity, kills his adversary in order to save himself from death or great bodily harm.

The conditions under which a homicide is excusable on the ground of self-defense are:

1. In a sudden affray, the threatened party must retreat as far as he can with safety before taking his adversary's life (in some jurisdictions this rule is applied to justifiable self-defense, where a person is feloniously assaulted, being without fault himself, while other jurisdictions hold that retreat is not necessary in such case).
2. The defendant slayer must not have been the aggressor, or have otherwise provoked the difficulty.

Some states have abolished the distinction between justifiable and excusable homicide and have classed all homicide in self-defense as justifiable.

Under the common law if a person feloniously assaults another with intent to kill him or inflict great bodily harm, the person so threatened, being without fault himself, may stand his ground and kill his assailant, if it is necessary to do so in order to save himself from death or great bodily harm, and the homicide will be justifiable, as distinguished from excusable, self-defense. Thus a woman may kill a man to prevent him from committing a rape upon her. And, if necessary, a person may kill another to prevent an attempted robbery. In these cases the homicide is justifiable because it is committed in order to prevent a felony.

The classic United States Supreme Court statement was made by Mr. Justice Holmes in *Brown v. United States,* 256 U.S. 335, 41 Sup. Ct. 501, in this passage:

> Concrete cases or illustrations stated in the early law in conditions very different from the present, like the reference to retreat in Coke, Third Inst 55, and elsewhere, have had a tendency to ossify into specific rules without much regard for reason. . . .
>
> Many respectable writers agree that if a man reasonably believes that he is in immediate danger of death or grievous bodily harm from his assailant he may stand his ground and that if he kills him he has not exceeded the bounds of lawful self-defense. That has been the decision of this Court. . . . Detached reflection cannot be demanded in the presence of an uplifted knife. Therefore in this Court, at least, it is not a condition of immunity that one in that situation should pause to consider whether a reasonable man might not think it possible to fly with safety or to disable his assailant rather than to kill him.

Excusable homicide in self-defense differs from justifiable homicide in self-defense at common law in that the parties are engaged in an "affray" or mutual combat so that both are deemed at fault. In such a situation the homicide is merely excused and not justified. It is called homicide *se defendo,* "on a sudden affray." The affray may arise in a number of different ways. Where a person is assaulted without felonious intent, and engages in a combat with his assailant, in the course of which it becomes necessary to kill his adversary in order to save himself from death or great bodily harm, and he does so, after retreating as far as he can with safety, he is regarded, according to the common law, as being to some extent at fault, and the homicide is not justifiable, but it is excusable. Apart from the duty to retreat, the slayer holds the same status as in the case of justifiable self-defense. The affray may arise in various ways: from resenting and returning a blow, or from resenting insulting words, or from resisting a trespass on land or goods, or from resisting an unlawful arrest. None of these provocations justify or excuse a homicide, and some of them do not mitigate or reduce it to manslaughter. If, however, in any of these cases it becomes necessary for one of the parties to take the other's life to save himself from death or great bodily harm, and he does so, the homicide is excusable, except as described in subsequent chapters in this volume.

Below is a summary of selected statutory provisions dealing with justifiable homicide in self-defense situations.

Force is Justifiable

Does not amount to an assault or battery when necessary to prevent commission of an offense. ARIZ. § 13-246.

May be used to break open a house to prevent the

commission of a felony therein. N.C. § 15-43.

Where it reasonably appears to be in necessary self-defense. ARK, §§ 41-2231, 41-2235; COLO. §§ 40-2-13, 40-2-14; ILL. c. 38, § 366; NEV. §§ 10076, 10077; GA. §§ 26-1011, 26-1012.

When resisting any attempt to murder such person (the slayer). FLA. § 782.02; KAN. § 21-404; MISS.§ 2218; MO. § 559.040; N.M. § 40-24-13; N.D. § 12-2705; OKL. t. 21, § 733; S.D. § 13.2003.

When resisting an attempt to commit a felony on the slayer. MINN. § 619.29; NEV. § 200.160; N.Y. § 1055; ORE. § 163.100; WASH. § 9.48.170; ALASKA § 65-4-10.

When it is committed in resisting an attempt to murder any person, or to commit a felony, or to do some great bodily injury on any person. ARIZ. § 13-462; CAL. § 197; IDAHO § 18-4009; MONT. § 94-2513; UTAH § 76-30-10; PUERTO RICO t. 33, § 641.

When committed in the reasonable belief that such action is necessary to prevent an entrance, in a violent manner, into a habitation for the purpose of offering violence to any person therein. All the statutes in 12. plus: ARK. § 41-2234; COLO. § 40-2-13; GA. § 26-1011; ILL. c. 38, § 366; NEV. § 200.120.

When committed under a reasonable apprehension of a design to commit, and imminent danger of the commission of, a felony or great bodily injury on:

(a) the slayer, or his wife, husband, parent, child, master, mistress, or servant. ARIZ. § 13-462; IDAHO § 18-4009; CAL. § 197; MONT. § 94-2513; UTAH § 76-30-10; PUERTO RICO t. 33 § 641; N.D. § 12-2705; OKL. t. 21 § 733; S.D. § 13.2003.
(b) same plus brother. N.M. § 40-24-13.
(c) same plus brother, and sister minus mistress. MINN. § 619.29.
(d) same plus apprentice. KAN. § 21-404.

(e) same plus brother, sister, aunt, uncle, nephew, niece, and apprentice. Mo. § 559.040.
(f) same plus grandparent, mother-in-law, father-in-law, son-in-law, daughter-in-law, grandchild, sister, brother, uncle, aunt, nephew, niece, guardian and ward. FLA. § 782.02.
(g) same minus master, mistress or servant, plus brother, sister, or any person in his presence or company. NEV. § 200.160; N.Y. § 1055; WASH. § 9.48.170.

To prevent the commission of a felony on the slayer, or his husband, wife, parent, child, master, mistress or servant. ORE. § 163.100; ALASKA § 65-4-10.

In the just and necessary defense of his life, or the life of his or her husband, wife, parent, child, brother, sister, master, servant, guardian or ward. VT. § 8245.

In self-defense, or in the defense of his or her husband, wife, parent, child, brother, sister, master, mistress or servant. N.J. § 2A:113-6.

When committed under a reasonable apprehension of a design to commit, and imminent danger of the commission of, a felony or great bodily injury on the slayer or any other person. MISS. § 2218.

When committed in self-defense under a reasonable apprehension of imminent danger of loss of life or great bodily harm; or in defense of others under the reasonable apprehension that the other party could justify killing in self-defense. LA. §§ 14:20, 14:22.

When committed in necessary defense of his own life, his family or property, or in legal defense of illegal proceedings against his wife, his family or himself. N.M. § 40-24-11.

In defense of the person or reputation of parents or children. GA. § 26-1015.

Opposition to what they did

- they bullet chems → matter of individual self-defense

- they used illegal force → see U.N. stipulations for international self-defense. (a party try to regain their homeland)

  → though poem

① nation must exhaust all alternative means of protection → they had no voice lawsuit to
  no desire to engage
  wish to put blame on the lib
  ② means must justify ends →
     (see notes on 47)
  ③ danger must be unacceptable. (no they mis remedied)

[try/alternative protect human rights]

- bombed places who were just out for money and cars

() they settled for less money → In their report you can see they want are their human rights.

Chapter 2

THE PRINCIPLES OF SELF—DEFENSE IN OUTLINE

Where a person is without fault and is either attacked, or in imminent fear of being attacked, such person may use reasonable force to defend against such attack. If the attack is with *deadly force* the majority rule is that the one attacked may defend with *deadly force* if deemed reasonable under the circumstances. The minority rule requires that the one attacked retreat if there is a safe means of doing so, unless the victim is in his own home or "castle."

To rely on the *justification* self-defense, one must first prove that he *is without fault* in causing the attack on him, the exception being where the defender first started the attack on another, then withdrew and gave notice of withdrawal by words or conduct. The rationale is that if one is to invoke the justification of self-defense, he must be innocent in connection with the encounter. But if the one attacked was actually the first to start the affray, he can exercise his right to self-defense upon complete withdrawal providing that the withdrawal is communicated in some reasonable fashion to the other.

Examples

D attacks V with a club. V, in defending himself from the attack, pulls a knife and threatens D with it. D, to stop V from causing harm, shoots him. D is not privileged or justified in harming V since D was at fault in starting the encounter.

D attacks V with a club. V, in defending himself from the unlawful attack, pulls a knife and threatens

D with it. D, upon seeing the knife throws away the club and says: "O.K., let's quit." V, seeing this, stalks D and tries to stab him. D, about to be stabbed, and having no way to retreat, shoots V. D is justified in defending himself from serious bodily harm because after the good faith withdrawal, V became the aggressor.

For one to rely on the justification of self-defense, *he must reasonably and honestly believe that he is in imminent danger of being harmed by the other.* If this belief is reasonable and in good faith, then the right of self-defense arises even if the belief turns out to be erroneous. If the one who thinks he is being attacked does not act reasonably in so believing, the acts committed in self-defense will not be justified and any killing resulting therefrom may be voluntary manslaughter rather than murder. And, if the one who acts in self-defense does so because of a threat of *future harm,* acts committed in self-defense will not be justified. (But see Chapter 6, "The Battered Wife Syndrome and the Imperfect Right of Self-Defense.).

Examples

D, walking down a dark street, is frightened by V running toward her. Based on this fear, D stabbed V, who in fact had no intention whatever of harming D. If the belief by D is unreasonable under the circumstances, D cannot rely upon the justification of self-defense.

D is walking down a lonely street and is confronted by V, who attempts to scare D by rushing toward her with a plastic non-operative gun shouting, "I'm going to kill you." D, being fearful that V would take her life, strikes V. If this belief by D is reasonable, D is justified in taking self-defensive measures. Whether such belief and action by D is reasonable would be a question for the jury.

V told D, "I'm going to beat you the next time I see you in this city." Fearful that V, in the future, would carry out this threat, D strikes V. D is not justified because V's threat was that of a future danger and there was no *imminent* danger. (But again, see Chapter 6).

In cases where the attacker makes a *nondeadly* attack, to rely on the justification of self-defense, one may use only that amount of force which is deemed to be reasonable, considering the circumstances. (See Appendix A, Model Penal Law, Section 3.11, "definitions.") Generally, therefore, one is not justified in using *deadly force* to prevent a *non-deadly* attack. What is a proportional response under the circumstances is usually an issue for the jury.

Examples

V, having disliked D for some time, wished to embarrass D at a party. To carry out this plan, V attempted to slap D in the face. To prevent this, D struck V on the head with a heavy case, causing V to be seriously injured. The force used by D is unreasonable, thus D is not justified in harming V on the basis of self-defense. If D had grabbed V to prevent the technical battery, the force used to restrain V would be reasonable and thereby justified.

V attempted to slap D in an offensive but non-harmful manner. To prevent this, D grabbed V and tried to restrain her. V, in pulling away, fell and struck her head, causing an injury from which V dies.

Since the force used by D was reasonable, D is not criminally liable even though V died.

Where a *deadly* attack is made, the one attacked may stand his ground or be required to retreat, depending on the jurisdiction. In the majority of states it is held that even if there is a safe means of escape, the person subjected to a *deadly* attack, *i.e.,* an attack threatening death or serious bodily harm, is not required to retreat, but may stand his ground and use deadly force to repel the attack if the use of deadly force is reasonable under the circumstances. However, in the minority of states (See Appendix A, Model Penal Code, Section 3.04, (2)(A)) the person subjected to a deadly attack must "retreat to the wall" before using deadly force if there is a reasonably safe method of escape from the danger, unless:

(a) The one attacked is in his home or dwelling, in which case he may stand his ground;
(b) Or, in some cases, the one attacked is subjected to a dangerous felony, *e.g.,* robbery;
(c) Or, in some cases, where the one attacked is trying to arrest the attacker in a *lawful* manner.

One is not required to retreat in any jurisdiction unless there is a safe method of retreating. Thus, if the one being attacked does not know of any safe retreat route, or if to retreat would increase his chances of harm, there is no retreat requirement.

Examples

V, holding a gun in his hand, confronted D on the street and says, "I'm going to kill you!" D, to prevent being killed, pulls a gun and shoots V. D is justified in doing so in the no-retreat jurisdiction. In the *retreat* jurisdictions, D would be justified in doing so if he had no safe means of escape. And, in the *retreat* jurisdictions, D would not have to retreat if he was in his home or "castle."

The chapters which follow discuss in detail the theories of self-defense presented here in outline. It should be noted that this volume deals with the defense of self-defense in the criminal law and not in torts. There are, however substantial if not complete similarities in much of the law of self-defense in these two divisions of the law, criminal and civil. A reading of the Restatement of Torts dealing with self-defense will bear this out.

For the purpose of a viable presentation of this topic of the law of self-defense, the focus of this study is criminal liability.

Chapter 3
THE AGGRESSOR'S RIGHT TO SELF-DEFENSE

As a general rule, when one is the aggressor in an encounter with another (i.e., one who provokes or initiates the encounter) such person may not avail himself of the defense of self-defense. The rationale for this is that since the aggressor's victim, defending himself against the aggressor, is using lawful, not unlawful force, then the force defended against must be unlawful force, for self-defense. There are, however, two situations in which an aggressor may *justifiably* defend himself:

1. A nondeadly aggressor (i.e., one who begins an encounter, using only his fists or some nondeadly weapon) who is met with deadly force in defense may justifiably defend himself against the deadly attack. When the aggressor's victim uses deadly force against nondeadly aggression, he is using unlawful force.
2. An aggressor who in good faith effectively withdraws from any further encounter with his victim (and to make an effective withdrawal he must notify the victim or at least take reasonable steps to notify him) is restored to his right of self-defense.

In *Rowe v. United States,* 164 U.S. 546, 17 S.Ct. 172, the aggressor, after kicking at the other, stepped back and leaned against a counter, not in an attitude for personal conflict; the Court held the jury should have determined whether this was intended to be, and could reasonably be interpreted to be, a withdrawal in good faith from further controversy. The Oregon Supreme Court in *State v. Broadhurst,* 184 Or. 178, 196 P.2d 407, said of good faith withdrawal that an aggressor must bring home to the other his intention to withdraw "in such a way that the adversary, as a reasonable man, must have known that the assault was ended." This statement is typical of the numerous ambiguous statements among the courts as to whether actual notice is required.

There are some decisions which hold that one who is himself the aggressor, or who otherwise brings on or provokes a fight, whether by acts or words, will not be excused for afterwards killing his adversary in self-defense, even though he may not have been actuated by malice in bringing on the difficulty. But most cases reject this view and uphold the doctrine outlined earlier, that one who commits an assault *without malice, or otherwise provokes a difficulty without malice,* and thereby brings about a conflict, may withdraw from the conflict, and if he does so in good faith, and in such an unequivocal manner as to show his adversary that he desires to withdraw, and his adversary follows him, and attempts to kill him or do him great bodily harm, he has the same right of self-defense as if he had not originally been the aggressor.

If, however, such an aggressor does not withdraw or offer to withdraw, he cannot successfully plead self-defense, but will be guilty of at least manslaughter.

It has been held that one caught in the act of adultery with another's wife, being attacked by the husband is not privileged to kill in self-defense. And if one resists an attempt to lawfully arrest him and kills the official in so doing he cannot set up self-defense.

The exercise of a legal right will rarely be held a provocation sufficient to deprive an aggressor of his right of self-defense even though he has reason to expect a conflict will result and arms himself accordingly.

The Model Penal Code (see Appendix B) denies justification for the use of deadly force if the accused, with the purpose of causing death or bodily harm, provoked the use of force against himself in the same encounter. The *Comments* dealing with this Section 3.04 (2)(b)(i) describes this case:

> "A attacks B with his fists; B defends himself and knocks A down, then starts to batter A's head savagely against the floor. A manages to rise and, since B is still attacking him and A now reasonably fears that if he is thrown again he will be killed, he uses a knife. B is killed or seriously wounded.
>
> ". . .the solution under the Code provisions is as follows:
>
> "B is entitled to defend himself against A's attack but only to the extent of using moderate, non-deadly force. He exceeds the bounds of necessary force, however, when, reducing A to helplessness he batters his head on the floor. Since this excessive force is, in its turn, unlawful, A is entitled to defend himself against it and, if he believes that he is then in danger of death or serious bodily harm without apparent opportunity for safe retreat, to use his knife in self-protection. Thus A is criminally liable for his initial battery on B but not for the ultimate homicide or wounding.
>
> "This conclusion - that an initial aggressor is accountable for his original unlawful use of force but not for his defense against a disproportionate return of force by his victim - is surely not unreasonable on its face. There is, however, much authority, both common law and statutory, demanding that a person claiming self-defense be free from fault in bringing on the difficulty. But the principle is not on the whole unqualified. The original aggressor is usually deemed to have a right of self-defense which is 'imperfect'; before it may be exercised he must give notice of his

wish to desist from the struggle and attempt to withdraw.

"The forfeiture rule thus serves primarily to impose a duty of desistance and retreat on the person who initiates a fight, a result which is of course desirable in a jurisdiction which does not impose that duty generally as a pre-condition of resort to deadly force. If such a duty is imposed in general, however, the need for such a special rule does not appear. So long as the assailant's victim employs moderate force in self-protection, it is not unlawful; the original assailant cannot, therefore, claim a privilege for a response in kind. The problem arises only when the victim transforms the necessity by answering moderate with deadly force. If in such a case there is no opportunity for withdrawal and safe retreat, we do not think the fact of the original minor aggression warrants the denial of a privilege to defend against deadly force; the initial aggressor can and ought to be convicted of assault.

"On this analysis the only case that calls for special treatment in the draft is that where the actor provokes a struggle (whether by assault, battery or insult or other means) with the positive purpose that the outcome shall be the death of his victim or his serious bodily harm. In this situation (the Code) provides that the fomenter of the struggle is deprived of his privilege of self-defense. Even here, the forfeiture is limited to the 'same encounter', implying that the assailant will regain his privilege of self-defense by so far breaking off the struggle that any renewal by the other party can be viewed as a distinct engagement."

Chapter 4
THE ISSUE OF RETREAT

"A true man, who is without fault, is not obliged to fly from an assailant who by violence or surprise maliciously seeks to take his life, or to do him enormous bodily harm." These words of the Supreme Court of Ohio were quoted with approval and followed by the United States Supreme Court in 1895. Two years later the same court sustained a charge to the jury to the effect that "if he is attacked by another in such a way as to denote a purpose to take away his life, or to do him some bodily harm . . . he may lawfully kill the assailant . . . provided he use all the means in his power to otherwise save his own life or prevent the intended harm, such as retreating as far as he can, or disabling him without killing him, if it be in his power." These contradictory views held by the same court at about the same time, have pretty evenly divided the jurisdictions in this country ever since.

In many if not most jurisdictions an innocent victim is under no duty to retreat even if he knows that he could do so with complete impunity,

The Model Penal Code *(see Appendix B)* reached a contrary conclusion with respect to the use of deadly force, concluding that most citizens would, in a moment of quiet reflection subsequent to the violent confrontation, prefer to have suffered the temporary ignominy of retreating rather than to have taken a human life. The Code does not, however, require a victim to retreat from his dwelling place or place of work. Nor need he retreat if he is assaulted in his dwelling by another person whose dwelling it is also.

In *People v. Lenkovich,* 394 Mich. 117, 229 N.W.2d 298, the defendant was convicted of murdering her husband during an altercation in their home. The judgment was reversed because the trial judge had instructed on the need to retreat:

> "We hold that when an attack occurs in one's home by an assailant who is not an intruder but who has a right to be on the premises, an assailed who is without fault need not 'retreat to the wall' before defending herself. In other words, the given instruction is improper in a situation where both the assailed and the assailant have an equal right, within limits, to stand their ground . . . While we recognize that there is a split of authority throughout the country in the applicability of the duty to retreat when the assailant and the assailed share the same living quarters, we agree with the reasoning of Judge Cardozo in *People v. Tomlins,* 213 N.Y. 240, 243-244, 107 N.E. 496, 497. In *Tomlins,* Judge Cardozo reasoned: 'It is not now, and never has been the law that a man assailed in his own dwelling is bound to retreat. If assailed there, he may stand his ground and resist the attack. He is under no duty to take to the fields and the highways, a fugitive from his own home . . . The rule is the same whether the attack proceeds from some other occupant or an intruder. It was so adjudged in *Jones v. State,* 76 Ala. 8, 14. 'Why,' it was there inquired, 'should one retreat from his own house, when assailed by a partner or cotenant, any more than when assailed by a stranger who is lawfully upon the premises? Whither shall he flee, and how far, and when may he be permitted to return?'"

Real exceptions to the original concept have appeared in the form of additional places from which no retreat is required. They create an "enlarged castle," so to speak. No enlargement was involved in the holding in regard to a roomer. His room is his dwelling place and therefore he is under no obligation to retreat if attacked in his room, although if attacked in another part of the house he must (under the retreat rule) retreat to his room, if he can in safety, before using deadly force, at least if the assailant is the owner or another occupant in the building.

There has been a tendency to enlarge the "castle" concept if this word is used figuratively to mean all places from which the innocent victim of a murderous assault is not required to retreat, before resorting to deadly force, in a retreat rule jurisdiction. There has been a definite trend in the direction of holding that a man is no more obliged to retreat from his place of business than from his dwelling. And this has been extended to include the private driveway leading to the place of business of a garage owner, and even to the open field if that is where the man works. Some courts have held that the privilege is available whenever the innocent victim is on his own premises at the time.

What appears to be the greatest extension of the "castle" in a retreat rule jurisdiction is found in South Carolina. A man is in his "castle" there not only if he is in his home or place of business, including an employee while working at his place of employment, but also if "on property owned or lawfully owned by him." This is true also when he is at his club. "A man is no more bound to allow himself to be run out of his rest room than his workshop." It is not true, however, merely because he is on a public highway. Nor does it apply to an employee who is at his place of employment at other than regular hours and not for any purpose connected with his employment.

The "castle" of his host becomes that also of his guest while the latter is present in that capacity. The guest is therefore under no more obligation to retreat than his host if attacked by an intruder. If the assailant should be another guest the legal view is that one occupant has attacked another occupant of the same "castle." On this point the retreat rule jurisdictions are not in agreement. A number of cases have held that there is not greater duty to retreat from another occupant than from an outsider, but other cases have denied the special privilege in such a situation.

Courts which have adopted the no retreat rule, often under the erroneous impression that this required departure from the English common law, have shown little tendency to change this stand. The other courts, as indicated, have shown an inclination to enlarge the "castle" concept, sometimes to the point of going over entirely to the other position.

The prevailing view, then, is that a victim may stand his ground and use deadly force if this reasonably seems necessary to save himself. Again, the theory is that liberty itself is threatened if a law-abiding citizen can be forced from a place where he has a right to be. But this extraordinary privilege is not available to an *aggressor.* The person who started the encounter with an *unlawful* exchange of blows enjoys no such position. He is in no sense blameless. But if he started, or joined in, the contest with no thought of causing death or great bodily harm, his fault in doing so is entirely overshadowed if the other wilfully changes it to a deadly encounter. In such a situation he has not entirely forfeited his privilege of self-defense. If he kills without availing himself of an obviously safe retreat he is guilty of manslaughter. If he retreats as far as he can in reasonable safety, he may use deadly force if this seems reasonably necessary to save himself from death or great bodily harm. And if as a result of the suddenness and fierceness of the change in nature of the encounter there is no reasonable opportunity to retreat, he may resort to deadly force where he is. And where both parties are in the wrong, neither is privileged to use deadly force without retreating.

Where one starts or willingly engages in an encounter with "malice aforethought," he is in a still worse position. Though he retreats as far as he can and then kills the other as the only possible means of saving his own life he is held guilty of murder. "Cases of mutual combat are those in which this duty of 'retreating to the wall' oftenest appears. Two men being in the wrong, neither can right himself except by 'retreating to the wall'".

However, even the murderous assailant has not necessarily forfeited his privilege of self-defense permanently. He has forfeited it for the moment. He cannot reacquire it by retreat to the wall. Nothing short of withdrawal will restore this privilege. This means that he must bring his attack to an end. And if he is not able to get away from the other, he must in some way convey to him the information that the fight is over. If the circumstances are such that he cannot do so, it is his own misfortune for bringing such a predicament upon himself. Without meeting the requirements of *retreat* or *withdrawal* (whichever may be applicable to the particular case), no one can raise the doctrine of self-defense when he himself has brought about the situation.

The Minority Retreat Rule

A large number of states have adopted the *retreat rule* as dintinguished from the prevailing *no-retreat rule*. While the application has been considerably whittled away by exceptions, the underlying position was to be summarized by the Harvard legal scholar of criminal law, Beale, in a classic law review article published in the Harvard Law Review in 1906, *Retreat from a Murderous Assault:* Even the innocent victim of a murderous assault must elect an obviously safe retreat, *if available,* rather than resort to deadly force unless (1) he is in his "castle" at the time, or his assailant is (2) one he is lawfully attempting to arrest or (3) a robber. The American Law Institute, adopting this position in general with a clear understanding of its status as a minority view, did not include the third exception. (See appendix B)

Corpus Jurisprudence Second summarizes this principle in the law of self-defense by stating that under no view is it the law that the right of self-defense does not arise until accused has done everything in his power to avoid the necessity of killing. Nor is it neccessary that there be an absolute lack of means of escape. If none was known or apparent to the accused at the time it is sufficient. And where the accused, acting on appearances, honestly and reasonably believes that he cannot retreat without increasing his peril, he may justifiably kill in his own defense, even though as a matter of fact, a retreat would not have endangered his personal safety. The question is not whether the jury believes, but whether the accused believed and had reasonable grounds to believe, that he had no safe, or apparently safe, means of protecting himself other than the slaying of his adversary.

Chapter 5
THE CONCEPT OF "FORCE" IN SELF-DEFENSE

Like the common law, the statutes among the states distinguish between the victim's right to use *non-deadly* force and *deadly* force in self-defense.

Which force, deadly or non-deadly, a victim can use in self-defense depends on the nature of the harm threatened. As a practical matter, however, this principle almost always limits a victim to respond in kind to the force used or threatened by the aggressor.

Non-deadly Force

A person who is himself free from fault is privileged to use non-deadly force in self-defense under three conditions; (1) He reasonably believes the other intends to commit an assault upon him, or unlawfully to imprison him, and this belief has been brought about by the other party's conduct. (2) That the defensive force is not unreasonable in view of the harm which it is intended to prevent. And (3) that the defender reasonably believes he cannot avoid the threatened harm without using defensive force or giving up some right or privilege.

An innocent person in this situation is under no obligation to retreat rather than use non-deadly force in his defense. He may stand his ground and defend himself where he is.

One may also use non-deadly force to defend himself against bodily harm which he reasonably believes to be immediately threatened by the negligent conduct of the other party. But he should yield ground rather than use force to avoid harm which he realizes is unintentional.

Deadly force is not privileged in defense against non-deadly force. For example, one must submit to a blow on the ear and seek redress in the courts if he is unable to prevent it by means other than resort to deadly force. If homicide should result it would not be less than manslaughter. If there is a great disparity between the two parties, death or great bodily harm is possible without any weapon, so that circumstances may justify deadly force to repel such an attack.

But unintentional homicide resulting from force which was neither intended nor likely to cause death or great bodily harm must be distinguished. If the blow itself was privileged, death unexpectedly and unintentionally resulting is *excusable*. It has been held that to avoid being choked to death, one may stab a stronger opponent.

An unlawful arrest is an unlawful trespass and according to common law it may be resisted by any non-deadly force which reasonably seems necessary to retain or regain the liberty of the person arrested. If, however, the unlawful arrest is attempted under circumstances which obviously threaten no more than a very temporary deprivation of liberty, the use of deadly force is not privileged. But if the unlawful manner of the arrest reasonably leads the arrested victim to reasonably believe that he is the victim of a murderous assault, or of kidnappers, homicide committed by him will not be criminal if he uses no more force than reasonably appears to be necessary under the circumstances.

Deadly Force

Deadly force is usually defined as force (a) which its user uses with intent to cause death or serious bodily harm to another or (b) which he knows creates a substantial risk of death or serious bodily injury to the other. (See Appendix B, Model Panel Code 3.11(2)). One therefore uses deadly force if he fires at another with intent to kill or do him serious bodily injury, though he

iolence offered to person. ARIZ. § 13-246; N.D. § 1
; OKL. t. 21 § 643; S.D. § 13.2402.

is not unlawful whenever used by a party about to
red or another helping him, in preventing an offen
inst his person. MONT. § 94-605; N.Y. § 246; WAS
11.040; ALASKA § 66-22-1.

Resistance sufficient to prevent an offense again
e's person or family, or to prevent an offense against
rd party, may be made. ARIZ. § 13-1205; CAL. §§ 69
4; IDAHO §§ 19-202. 19-203; IOWA §§ 691.1, 691.
ONT. §§ 94-5002, 94-5003; TENN. §§ 38-102, 38-10
TAH §§ 77-2-2, 77-2-3.

actually misses him completely or causes him only minor bodily injury.

In determining how much force one may use in self-defense, the law recognizes that the amount of force which he may justifiably use must be reasonably related or proportional to the threatened harm which he seeks to avoid. As it was pointed out earlier, one may justifiably use *nondeadly* force against another in self-defense if he reasonably believes that the other is about to inflict unlawful bodily harm (it need not be death or serious bodily harm) upon him (and also believes that it is necessary to use such force to prevent it). Under these circumstances, then, he is not guilty of assault (if he merely threatens to use the nondeadly force or if he aims that force at the other but misses) or battery (if he injures the other by use of that (force).

He may justifiably use *deadly force* against the other in self-defense, however, only if he *reasonably* believes that the other is about to inflict unlawful death or serious bodily harm upon him and also that it is necessary to use deadly force to prevent it.

As long as the defendant's belief is reasonable, he may be mistaken in his belief and still have the defense. It has been held that one may be justified in shooting to death an adversary who, having threatened to kill him, reaches for his pocket as if he were going to draw out a gun, though it later appears that he had no gun and that he was only reaching for a handkerchief. A very early but still cited case, *Shorter v. People,* 2 N.Y. 193 (1849), stated that one is justified in killing another in self-defense when *reasonably* apprehending harm, "although it may afterwards turn out that the appearances were false, and was *in fact* neither design to do him serious injury nor danger that it would be done."

Mr. Justice Holmes, in appraising the situation one

may, under the circumstances, be reasonable though mistaken since, to put it in a much-quoted expression: "Detached reflection cannot be demanded in the presence of an uplifted knife."

In *Grainger v. State,* 13 Tenn. 459 (1830), an overpowering bully threatened the defendant, a timid and cowardly man, with violence, intending a battery but not to kill. It was reasoned that if the defendant thought himself in danger of great bodily harm from the bully, the killing was in self-defense. *Vigil v. People,* 143 Colo. 328, 353 P.2d 82 (1960) held that an instruction that the right to self-defense is based on what reasonable persons would do under similar circumstances was held error. The court stated that animals, who cannot reason, instinctively act in self-preservation, so self-defense by mankind is not based upon the reasonable man concept.

Behind the reasoning in the cases which uphold the individual's reasonable belief is the proposition that one may act in self-defense not only when a reasonable person would so act, but when one with the particular qualities of the defender himself would do so. In short, a nervous, timid, easily-frightened man is not measured by the same standard as a stronger, braver man, On the other hand, an earlier case, *Teal v. State,* 22 Ga. 75 (1874), held as erroneous a defendant's requested instructions that "the fears of a coward would justify homicide." The court argued that the fears for self-defense must be those "of a reasonable man; reasonably courageous-reasonably self-possessed."

The Model Penal Code supports this view on the theory that there should be no conviction of a crime requiring intentional misconduct of one who is guilty of only negligence in making the unreasonable mistake. The Code requires only that the actor "believes" that the use of force is necessary.

Chapter 6
THE BATTERED WIFE SYNDROME AND THE IMPERFECT RIGHT OF SELF-DEFENSE

Courts apply the label "perfect" to the right of self-defense if the defense, having resulted in homicide, entitles the defendant to an aquittal, and "imperfect" if the defense merely reduces the grade of the offense to manslaughter.

The presence of all the four elements required to be present at the time of the killing described in the previous chapters give the defendant a "perfect" right of self-defense and requires a verdict of not guilty, not only as to the charge of murder in the first degree, but as to all lesser offenses as well.

If the defendant believed it was necessary to kill the deceased in order to save himself from death or great bodily harm and if the defendant's belief was reasonable, but the defendant was the aggressor or he used excessive force, the defendant has only an "imperfect" right of self-defense. Having lost the benefit of "perfect" self-defense, the defendant is guilty of at least manslaughter.

This so-called imperfect right of self-defense presents itself increasingly in cases where women kill in self-defense. This defense is often described as the *abused spouse's* defense. Women, abused spouses in particular, who kill in self-defense often do not fit the facts mold of the traditional self-defense concept.

Recognition of this special situation abused women find themselves in appeared in a Washington State Supreme Court decision, *State v. Wanrow*, 559 P.2d 548, reversing a felony murder and first degree assault conviction of a female defendant. In a yet rare, but emerging opinion, the court held that she was entitled to a self-

29

defense jury instruction that included the woman's perceptive. The court concluded that:

> The respondent was entitled to have the jury consider her actions in the light of her own perceptions of the situation, including those perceptions which were the product of our nation's long and unfortunate history of sex discrimination. Until such time as the effects of that history are eradicated, care must be taken to assure that our self-defense instructions afford women the right to have their conduct judged in the light of the individual handicaps which are the product of sex discrimination. To fail to do so is to deny the right of the individual woman involved to trial by the same rules which are applicable to male defendants.

Because the battered woman's use of deadly force may not have conformed to the traditional definitions, it was often necessary to offer a defense of insanity or diminished capacity in an attempt to explain the woman's actions. These choices forced the woman into a situation of having to face either a prison sentence or commitment to a mental institution for the act of defending herself.

It is often difficult for courts and attorneys to conceptualize how the self-defense plea can be asserted for the battered woman. First, the battered woman may kill at a time which does not appear reasonable outside the context of the battering relationship. However, the battered woman who acts in self-defense does so at a time *when she reasonably perceives her life to be in danger*. In such a situation her use of deadly force is justified. But a battered woman may kill the man when he is lying down or is asleep. In these situations, the woman is afraid that when the man gets up he will begin to batter her again, probably because he has told her that he would do so.

In a South Carolina case the defendant was charged

with murder in the death of her husband. He had given her a loaded shotgun, telling her that one of them was going to have to kill the other in order to resolve their abusive situation. He told her that she should be gone when he awoke, and then he went to the bedroom to go to sleep. Knowing that a beating was imminent and that she had no place to go, she followed him and shot him. She was acquitted on the charge of murder.

Women in these cases are afraid that if they try to leave, the man will come after her. Thus, although she may not be receiving an actual physical attack at the time, she nevertheless believes that her life is in imminent danger.

Another situation during which the battered woman uses deadly force occurs during the tension building phase of the battering cycle when the battering is not as severe as during the acute phase. Once again, her past experiences with this man influence her perceptions of what is happening at that time. She does not focus upon what is occurring at that moment, rather she is fearful of the harm she knows he is capable of inflicting upon her and she wants only to protect herself from that harm.

In defending the battered woman, defenses of justification are the most appropriate. The most effective of the defenses of justification is self-defense or self-protection, but other defenses may be applicable and necessary, including mental disease or defect, voluntary or involuntary intoxication, and extreme emotional disturbance. Such defenses may be important and helpful in mitigating or reducing the offense to a lesser degree if an aquittal appears unlikely.

In choosing the defense of self-protection in any self-defense case, entitlement to a self-defense instruction may become a crucial issue. The burden of proof is on the defendant to convince the jury by her evidence that the act, once committed, was excusable.

Instructions used in self-defense homicide cases usually define physical force, deadly physical force and serious physical injury. The issue therefore is, if any, whether deadly or non-deadly. The battered spouse defendant's facts may not fit the typical facts granting self-defense instructions, nor do the typical self-defense instructions fit her facts and needs. In her fact situation, the force or injury may be remote, or only anticipated, and thus not appear as *imminently deadly force* to the court and jurors. Typical self-defense instructions do not make allowance for such misfit facts, her perception of her situation, or psychological differences from her aggressor. For the battered woman defendant, one must request instructions which emphasize the physical circumstances which must be considered in evaluating and meeting the situation as the defendant did. Physical circumstances may generally include the strength and physical condition of the parties involved and the fact that women generally are not as able as men to defend themselves against an attack by a man. Factors such as pregnancy may affect the defendant's perception of the situation and her ability to protect herself. Legal writers dealing with this subject have been urged that menopause or Pre-Menstrual Syndrome may also have affected her emotional stability and state of mind.

An instruction allowing the jury to consider a history of the deceased's prior acts of violence against the defendant, defendant's knowledge as to the deceased's prior act of violence, are acknowledged to be a proper request.

A Kentucky court in an unreported case used an instruction embodying some of these principles. In that case the defendant spouse was acquitted on a murder charge. The defendant, a twenty-year-old mother of two young children, had suffered physical abuse from her husband. She shot and killed him as he stood several yards from her, taunting her. He had beaten her three days prior to the shooting, but had not actually touched her the evening of the shooting, nor was he armed. These facts did not fit the mold of the traditional self-defense case, but with an understanding and acknowledgment of the battered woman syndrome, the defendant's personality and the circumstances, a self-defense instruction was allowed:

> 1. "If at the time the defendant shot and killed Eugene Phillips (if she did so), she believed that Eugene Phillips was about to use such physical force against [her] as she reasonably believed, based upon a prior history of repeated and serious physical abuse, to be necessary in order to protect herself from death or serious physical injury.
> 2. Abused in this chapter, the term "mental disease or defect" does not include an abnormality manifested only by repeated criminal or otherwise antisocial conduct.
> 3. A defendant may prove mental disease or defect, as used in this section, in exculpation of criminal conduct."

The language used in this instruction which sets it apart from the standard self-defense instruction was the language which directed the jury to see the situation as the defendant perceived it. The jury instructions here recognized the spouse abuse defense approach by referring to the history of abuse. What this essentially means is an acceptance of the subjective test of a defendant's reasonable belief that she is confronting a serious and imminent bodily harm which justifies an act of self-defense. While many states have adopted the Model Penal Code which sanctions the subjective test in self-defense situations, only the most "enlightened" courts are actually applying it in the battered spouse cases where its use is probably most appropriate for achieving a just outcome.

This discussion should not lead the reader to conclude that the use of the battered woman syndrome to explain the reasonableness of a woman's perception of imminent danger means that there is a defense called the battered woman syndrome. Battering, or a history of abuse alone, does not justify a homicide.

The battered woman syndrome is not in or of itself a defense. The defense which is asserted is self-defense, not that the woman was a battered woman. What must be proved is that at the time of the incident, the woman reasonably perceived her life to be in imminent danger. The history of abuse does not justify the use of deadly force, but it does provide the woman with the knowledge to reasonably perceive that she is in imminent danger of death or great bodily harm. Testimony relating to the battered woman syndrome is not offered to establish a novel defense, rather, it is offered to assist a jury in assessing how the syndrome related to the defendant's claim of self-defense. In other words, the defense attorney and the defendant herself must convince the jury that her perceptions and actions at the time of the homicide fulfilled the legal requirements of self-defense.

Chapter 7
THE BERNHARD GOETZ CASE

No study of the law of self-defense as it exists today would be complete without some discussion of the Bernhard Goetz case in New York City. This case has probably brought more public attention to this field of law than any case in recent memory.

Goetz wounded four teenagers in a New York City subway car on December 22, 1984. He was carrying an unlicensed pistol. He contended that he feared they would rob him. The case focused national and even international attention on the question of when a citizen is justified in using deadly force in self-defense.

The key issue in the case as it went through a series of appeals was his justification in shooting the four youths, one of whom has been left paralyzed from the waist down.

The prosecution contended that he should be judged by whether he acted as some hypothetical "reasonable man" might have in the same situation. Mr. Goetz's attorneys argued that the case should hinge on whether the defendant's response to the situation was reasonable *for him*. In other words, whether the *objective* or the *subjective* test is applicable under New York State law.

The New York Court of Appeals reinstated charges of attempted murder and assault against Goetz after a series of lower courts dismissed the charges on the ground that there were prosecution errors in instructions to the grand jury about the legal justification of self-defense. New York's highest court held that the lower court rulings had misinterpreted the state statute dealing with the legal justification of self-defense.

In its discussion, the court said the reasonable-man standard, although perhaps ambiguous in its wording in the statute, was clearly the tradition of the law of New York State since 1829 and the intent of the Legislature when it revised the state's penal code in 1965.

The court acknowledged that subjective considerations could not be wholly ruled out, but said the reasonable-man rule should be the primary standard.

After the shootings a Manhattan grand jury indicted Goetz only on charges of weapons possession, for the unlicensed gun. A second grand jury, convened after the Manhattan District Attorney's office argued that it had new evidence, indicted Goetz on charges of attempted murder and assault, which carry a penalty of up to 15 years in prison.

That second indictment was restored by the Court of Appeals.

The case will be brought to trial after the publication of this volume. It will establish the facts in the case which in turn will determine the application of the New York law on the objective reasonable man test. The jury will decide whether the facts justified Goetz's response of deadly force.

Following are excerpts from the State Court of Appeals decision to reinstate attempted murder, assault and other charges against defendant Bernard Goetz. The decision was unanimous.

". . . In an order (the Criminal Term . . . held . . . that the prosecutor, in a supplemental charge elaborating upon the justification defense, had erroneously introduced an objective element into this defense by instructing the grand jury to consider whether Goetz's conduct was that of a 'reasonable man in /Goetz's/ situation.' The court . . . conclude that the statutory test for whether the use of deadly force is justified to protect a person should be wholly subjective, focusing entirely on the defendant's state of mind when he used such force.

"Article 35 of the Penal Law recognizes the defense of justification, which 'permits the use of force under certain circumstances.' Subdivision 1 of Penal Law Section 35.15 sets forth the general principles governing all such uses of force: 'A person may . . . use physical force upon another person when and to the extent he reasonably believes such to be necessary to defend himself or a third person from what he reasonably believes to be the use or imminent use of unlawful physical force by such other person.'

"Subdivision 2 sets forth further limitations with respect to 'deadly physical force': 'A person may not use deadly physical force upon another person under circumstances specified in Subdivision 1 unless (a) he reasonably believes that such other person is using or is about to use deadly physical force . . . or (b) he reasonably believes that such other person is committing or attempting to commit a kidnapping, forcible rape, forcible sodomy or robbery.'

"Because the evidence before the second grand jury included statements by Goetz that he acted to protect himself from being maimed or to avert a robbery, the prosecutor correctly chose to charge the justification defense in Section 35.15 to the grand jury.

"When the prosecutor had completed his charge, one of the grand jurors asked for clarification of the term 'reasonably believes.' The prosecutor responded by instructing the grand jurors that they were to consider the circumstances of the incident and determine 'whether the defendant's conduct was that of a reasonable man in the defendant's situation.' It is this response by the prosecutor-and specifically his use of 'a reasonable man'- which is the basis for the dismissal of the charges by the lower courts. As expressed repeatedly in the Appellate Division's plurality opinion, because Section 35.15 uses the term 'he reasonably believes,' the appropriate test, according to that court, is whether a defendant's beliefs and reactions were 'reasonable to him.'

"In 1961 the Legislature established a commission to undertake a complete revision of the Penal Law and the Criminal Code. Under Model Penal Code Section 3.04, a defendant charged with murder (or attempted murder) need only show that he 'believed that the (use of deadly force) was necessary to protect himself against death, serious bodily injury, kidnapping or forcible sexual intercourse' to prevail on a self-defense claim.

"The drafters of the new penal law adopted in large part structure and content of the Model Penal Code Section the 3.04, but, crucially, inserted the word 'reasonably' before 'believed.'

"The plurality below agreed with defendant's argument that the change in the statutory language from 'reasonable ground,' used prior to 1965, to 'he reasonably believes' in Penal Law 35.15 evidenced a legislative intent to conform to the subjective standard contained in Model Penal Code 3.04. This argument, however, ignores the plain significance of the insertion of 'reasonably.'

"We cannot lightly impute to the Legislature an intent to fundamentally alter the principles of justification to allow the perpetrator of a serious crime to go free simply because that person believes his actions were reasonable and necessary to prevent some perceived harm. To completely exonerate such an individual, no matter how aberrational or bizarre his thought patterns, would allow citizens to set their own standards for the permissible use of force. It would also allow a legally competent defendant suffering from delusions to kill or perform acts of violence with impunity, contrary to fundamental principles of justice and criminal law.

"We can only conclude that the Legislature retained a reasonableness requirement to avoid giving a license for such actions.

"Goetz... argues that the introduction of an objective element will preclude a jury from considering factors such as the prior experiences of a given actor and thus, require it to make a determination of 'reasonableness' without regard to the actual circumstances of a particular incident. This argument, however, falsely presupposes that an objective standard means that the background and other relevant characteristics of a particular actor must be ignored. To the contrary, we have frequently noted that a determination of reasonableness must be based on the 'circumstances' facing a defendant or his 'situation.'"

Davidson College Library

Davidson College Library

Chapter 8

SELF-DEFENSE IN INTERNATIONAL LAW

History

The right of national self-defense has existed since ancient times. The rules regarding self-defense have evolved from the rules governing warfare. In ancient civilizations, warfare was both frequent and "regulated." In ancient Greece, for example, any war had to be preceded by belligerency, or the war could not be justified. Ancient civilizations demonstrated evidence of the early emergence of a right of national self-defense.

Plato, although not an advocate of war, believed that wars fought on defensive grounds to forestall imminent or future attack were justified. The Romans followed a code of war that permitted aggressive actions for defensive purposes, in response to instigations such as the "violation of a treaty, . . . offenses committed against allies, . . . denial of neutrality, or desecration of sacred places." Similarly, the seventeenth century father of international law, Grotius, affirmed the natural right of national self-defense in the face of immediate and certain danger from an identified potential assailant even though no injury had yet occurred. Very much like the principle of the right of self-defense between individuals, Grotius affirmed the natural right of self-defense which "has its origins directly and chiefly in the fact that nature commits to each his own protection, not in the injustice or crime of the aggressor."

Early American leaders embraced a concept of national self-defense that included preemptive attacks. For Thomas Jefferson, this right lay at the foundation of good government because, he maintained, a nation's very existence depends upon it. The authors of the Federalist

Papers implicitly addressed national self-defense in their tracts advocating congressional discretion to raise armies in times of peace for defensive purposes. Alexander Hamilton argued that, if Congress were constitutionally prohibited from raising peace-time armies, the nation would be "incapacitated by its constitution to prepare for defense, before it was actually invaded," and the country would be forced to abstain from the policies "by which nations anticipate distant danger, and meet the gathering storm." Thus, Hamilton considered such a prohibition "contrary to the genuine maxims of a free government." James Madison discussed the futility of erecting "constitutional barriers to the impulse of self-preservation."

In the Monroe Doctrine of 1837, the United States declared its intention to invoke the right of anticipatory self-defense whenever a European nation attempted to interfere with or extended its colonial system to any independent nation on the American continents.

During the Canadian insurrection of 1837, sympathizers gathered near Buffalo, and a large number of Americans and Canadians encamped on the Canadian side of the boundary with apparent intention to aid the rebels. The *Caroline,* an American vessel which they used for supplies and communications, was boarded in an American port at midnight by an armed group, acting under orders of a British officer, who set the vessel on fire and let it drift over Niagra Falls. At least two persons were killed in the affair. The United States protested, while the British Government replied that the piratical character of the *Caroline* was established, that the American laws were not being enforced along the border, and that the destruction was an act of necessary self-defense. In 1841 MacLeod, a person who boasted of having taken part in the destruction, was arrested in New York and tried for murder. The British Government avowed responsibility for the destruction and demanded MacLeod's release. MacLeod was ultimately tried and acquitted on proof of an alibi. Secretary of State Webster and Lord Ashburton finally disposed of the case in 1912, Webster and Lord Ashburton finally disposed of the case in 1912, Webster admitting that the employment of force might have been justified by self-defense but denying that such necessity for its use existed. Lord Ashburton, though he maintained that the circumstances provided an excuse, apologized for the invasion of American territory. In his note of August 6, 1842, Webster said: "respect for the inviolable character of the territory of independent states is the most essential foundation of civilization. . . Undoubtedly it is just, that, while it is admitted that exceptions growing out of the great law of self-defense do exist, those exceptions should be confined to cases in which the 'necessity of that self-defense is instant, overwhelming, and leaving no choice of means, and no moment for deliberation.'" This definition is obviously drawn from the concept of the right of self-defense in domestic law; the cases are rare in which it would exactly fit an international situation.

But it is an accurate definition for international law in the sense that the exceptional right of self-defense can be exercised only if the end cannot be otherwise accomplished. In 1926, when League of Nations experts were studying the problems which would result from the application of sanctions under Article 16 of the Covenant, a Belgian jurist noted that "Legitimate defense implies the adoption of measures proportionate to the seriousness of the attack and justified by the imminence of the danger." As has been described in this volume as it deals with personal self-defense in the criminal law, when an individual is set upon by an armed thug who threatens his life, action is clearly required and it can be said that there is "no moment for deliberation." When a nation anticipates a threatened injury from another country or from a lawless band, there is usually opportunity for deliberation in the foreign or war office, and an officer on the spot does not act until he has received instructions from a higher command. Radio communication between the officer and his superiors can be taken as a counterpart of the impulses in the nervous system of the individual whose brain instructs his arm to strike.

When, in 1928, nations renounced war as an instrument of national policy (Kellogg-Briand Pact) and agreed that they would not seek to settle their disputes by other than peaceful means, the right of self-defense was expressly reserved. A United States statement declared that the proposed treaty did not in any way restrict or impair the right of self-defense. "That right is inherent in every sovereign state and is implicit in every treaty. Every nation is free at all times and regardless of treaty provisions to defend its territory from attack or invasion and it alone is competent to decide whether circumstances require recourse to war in self-defense."

Source of International Law of Self-Defense

The first source of international law is *international convention.* Since all signatories are bound by the terms of their conventions, the rules here are considered the most definitive source of international law. The clearest example of international convention is the United Nations Charter. The Charter imposes an important limitation on the use of force by United Nations members. Article 2, paragraph 4, provides: "All Members shall refrain in their international relations from the threat or use of force against the territorial integrity or political independence of any state, or in any other manner inconsistent with the Purposes of the United Nations."

However, the Charter expressly states in Article 51 that the remaining provisions of the Charter, including the limitation of Article 2, paragraph 4, in no way diminish the *inherent* right of self-defense against armed attack. Article 51 provides: "Nothing in the present Charter shall impair the inherent right of individual or collective self-defense if an armed attack occurs against a Member of the United Nations, until the Security Council has taken the measures necessary to maintain international peace and security. Measures taken by Members in the exercise of this right of self-defense shall be immediately reported to the Security Council and shall not in any way affect the authority and responsibility of the Security Council under the present Charter to take at any time such action as it deems necessary in order to maintain or restore international peace and security." This Article is, then, a "saving clause" designed to make clear that no other provision in the Charter can be interpreted to impair the inherent right of self-defense referred to in Article 51.

The second source of international law is *custom*. This encompasses two elements, the first of which is "a generalized repetition of similar acts by competent authorities." Custom derives from the *actions* of nations, actions which are essentially uniform and widespread. The second element is a shared sentiment that these actions are legally permissible. The practice must be generally perceived as required by law or at least as consistent with law. Among the various sources of customary law are diplomatic correspondence, executive decisions and practices, official policy statements, and treaties. Although these sources are not themselves law, they do evidence that legal rules of general application—in this case customary rules—may exist.

The third source of international law, characterized in the Statute of the International Court of Justice (which codifies the four sources of law) as "general principles of law recognized by civilized nations," reflects the influence of natural law theory. This source enables international tribunals to refer to rules that are common to various domestic legal systems. The distinguishing feature of this source of law is its reference to the basic legal principles shared by all nations with developed legal systems.

The fourth source of international law is the writings or opinions of courts and scholars. These judicial opinions may be those of national as well as international tribunals. In either case, however, the opinions serve only as evidence of law. The decisions of the International Court of Justice, for example, bind only the immediate parties to a dispute and have only persuasive, not precedential value. The writings of scholars constitute persuasive authority to the extent that the scholars have established reputations in thier fields.

Legal Principles for Invoking Self-Defense

The sources of international law together establish three standard elements necessary to assert the right of self-defense.

First, the threatened nation must exhaust all alternative means of protection. This means that the threatened nation must make diplomatic efforts to restore the status *quo ante,* for example, by attempting direct negotiations with the offending country or by appealing to the United Nations. The requirement to exhaust alternative means does not mean that the threatened nation must make continuous attempts to gain the offending nation's approval on a proposal it has explicitly rejected. The threatened nation must nevertheless make all reasonable efforts to avert the attack until the danger, or threat of danger, is virtually unavoidable and immediate.

Second, the defensive measure must be proportionate to the threatened danger. The various sources of international law describe proportionality alternatively as either inflicting no more damage than that inflicted by the initial injury of the offending state, or as remaining within the confines of moral notions of human rights, which require the avoidance of full-scale war and the restriction of force to that strictly necessary to eliminate the danger. The nation must direct its force only to the threat and not pursue other goals; it must avoid escalation by limiting the duration and severity of the strike. This would mean, for example, sporadic territorial incursions would not justify a full military invasion.

Third, the danger must be immediate. It is this element about which the sources of international law vary most. The definition of imminency has been subject to varying interpretations. Before the adoption of the United Nations Charter, customary international law supported a national right of self-defense. This right was broad enough to permit anticipatory action against "imminent" threats as well as defensive action in response to actual attacks, such as occurred in the *Caroline* case discussed earlier in this chapter.

Whether the United Nations Charter modified this international custom is the subject of debate among international judges and scholars. Article 51 of the Charter provides that the "inherent right" of self-defense against armed attack shall not be impaired by the Charter.

One view asserts that self-defense is justified only in response to an actual armed attack. This rests on the very language of the Article which provides that nothing shall impair the right of self-defense "if an armed attack occurs against a Member of the United Nations." The plain meaning would appear to permit self-defense only in response to an armed attack and not in anticipation of one. This is the restrictive view. A second restrictive argument interprets Article 51 in connection with Article 33, which obliges member nations to seek "peaceful means" to settle disputes. Read together, these two Articles would allow only "peaceful means" of dispute resolution and would mandate refraining from the unilateral use of force until the advent of an actual armed attack.

The broader interpretation of Article 51 permits some defensive strikes prior to actual offensive attacks. The counter-argument for a broad reading of the Charter is that Article 51 speaks in terms of a preservation of rights, stating that "nothing shall impair" the right to defend. There is nothing in the Charter that prohibits the defensive use of force in anticipation of immediate attack. The Charter is silent on that point.

When all is said and done, it appears that the elements for justifying self-defense in the criminal law as well as the rationale for permitting such self-preservation in the face of imminent attack, have essentially their counter-parts in the doctrine of self-defense in international law.

Epilogue

THE RIGHT OF SELF-DEFENSE: A QUESTION OF VALUES AND LAW

An individual is subjected to a violent attack; an individual finds himself threatened with serious and immediate violence. The right to life, or at least the right to physical security, is under challenge. Should the law favor the defender's interests at all times? Should an attacker forfeit his basic rights by making such an assault? Does the attacker's right to life and physical security warrant *any* legal protection? How highly should the state value this basic right, by comparison with other important social policies?

In any legal system, the law of self-defense explicitly or implicitly adopts a particular stance on these issues and embodies a more or less clear order of priority of values. Any criticism of the law as presently invoked must therefore be preceded by a consideration of the interests of each party involved (the defender, the attacker and the state) and of the values which ought to be protected.

What are the interests of an individual who falls victim to an unlawful attack? His essential interest, which some would regard as incapable of being overridden, lies in his own survival and physical integrity. If this interest is absolute when there is a realistic threat to his life, it becomes weaker as the seriousness of the harm threatened or inflicted diminishes. An individual who is attacked might also claim that he had an interest in ensuring that his attacker is punished, but there is an important distinction between assisting in the enforcement of the law and inflicting punishment. It is a mark of a civilized society that *punishment* may only be carried out by official agencies according to the law. The individual's interest is merged into the state's interest in the punishment of all persons duly proved to have broken the criminal law. For an individual to "take the law into his own hands," by inflicting summary punishment on his attacker is properly regarded a crime in itself.

Should the interests of the criminal attacker also be considered? There is little to support the view that a criminal loses all of his civil rights when he commits any offense. On the other hand, someone who makes a murderous attack on another must forfeit his right to life if this appears to be the only way in which the victim's life can be preserved.

When, however, his assault is less serious, the criminal's right to life remains protected and he merely loses his right to physical security: the defender's liberty to use force in self-defense overrides the criminal's normal right to physical integrity. But in all cases the criminal should retain the right not to be subjected to force which is neither necessary for his victim's defense nor necessary for any other lawful purpose which the defender starts to pursue. A criminal ought to be protected against excessive force and against any arbitrary treatment after his attack has been repelled.

The law must achieve a just and proper balance between the interests of defender and attacker, victim and criminal. This balance will reflect the state's own priority of values. The preservation of human life must rank high among state interests, and the interests in the minimization of physical violence, in the promotion of law enforcement and what has been termed "the suppression of private welfare" all have a bearing upon the justifiability of force. When there is an attack or threat of attack with deadly force, the problem of the extent to which the respective lives of attacker and defender should be protected by law arises. Where a situation does not present a clear choice between the lives of attacker and defender, the law should not hesitate to protect the life of the innocent rather than the life of the criminal attacker. Yet, how far should this protection be carried in a society which regards the right to life as fundamental? Surely the "choice of lives" situation only arises when the defender cannot (without physical danger to himself) avoid the use of serious violence.

A legal system which supports the maximum protection for *every* human life should provide that a person attacked ought if possible to avoid the use of violence, especially deadly force, against his attacker. This might be characterized as the "human rights" approach to self-defense. This approach, supported by the state interest in minimizing violence, would result in a duty to avoid the use of force where non-violent means of protection are reasonably open to the person attacked.

A different set of legal rules would result from what might be called a "stand fast" approach. While on a "human rights" approach a person attacked might be obliged to withdraw if this would protect him from further attack, the "stand fast" approach favors the liberty of a law-abiding citizen to stand his ground when confronted with an unlawful assault. Three reasons for supporting this approach can be offered: a show of strength might discourage a pending attack, it is wrong that a criminal should be able to require a law-abiding citizen to make a timid and dishonorable withdrawal, and beyond this a law which purports to curb the basic instinct towards self-preservation will prove unenforceable. A person attacked should therefore be entitled to stand fast and to repel force by force until that is no longer necessary for self-protection. From the "human rights" point of view, the drawback of this approach lies in its use of the concept of necessity. It is arguable that the use of force cannot be necessary if withdrawal is reasonably possible, and therefore the "stand fast" approach neglects to offer the maximum protection for the life and limb of the attacker. As a matter of fact, the "stand fast" approach appears to favor the law-abiding citizen's feelings of honor and self-respect at the expense of the criminal's right to life or physical security.

This view in relation to the use of non-serious force blurs the distinction between purely defensive force and the kind of punitive force we call "teaching him a lesson." Dicey's *Law of the Constitution,* one of the great classic studies in English law by one of the greatest English constitutional scholars, in an astute and sensitive discussion of the law of self-defense, described the dangers in this way:

> The rule which fixes the limit of the right of self-help must, from nature of things, be a compromise between the necessity, on the one hand, of allowing every citizen to maintain his rights against private wrongdoers, and the necessity, on the other hand, of suppressing private warfare. Discourage self-help, and loyal subjects become the slaves of ruffians. Over-stimulate self-assertion, and for the arbitrament of the courts you substitute the decision of the sword or the revolver.

Could it be contended that the "human rights" approach, with its emphasis on the avoidance of violence, would put law-abiding citizens at the mercy of ruffians? Might not the "stand fast" approach encourage individuals to take the law into their own hands? Opinions differ as to the realism of these fears today. In principle, however, the "human rights" approach may be defended on the grounds that it aims at maximum protection for every life, the minimization of violence and the suppression of private warfare, while the "stand fast" approach aims at maximum protection for the rights and liberties of the law-abiding citizen.

It is almost a matter of definition that law restricts the freedom of each individual to satisfy his wants and desires in any manner he wishes. The restrictive elements in law may be regarded as justifiable because and in so far as they are necessary to ensure the maximum freedom for each and every individual. Freedom *from* interference can only be preserved by restricting everyone's freedom *to* exercise power over others. Perhaps the most fundamental and universal restriction is that placed on the use of force by one individual against another. Widely as social and legal systems may vary in the extent to which they allow some forms of power (*e.g.,* the powers of persuasion) to be exercised, they unite in prohibiting the exercise of physical power by one citizen against another. Many natural inequalities may be allowed to run free, but all legal systems attempt to "equalize" human being to the extent of preventing resort to force by those who are minded and able to use this method of satisfying their desires. A prohibition on the use of force may therefore be regarded as one of the minimum conditions of social life. This, in turn, is bound up with recognition of the right to life and physical security as the most basic claim of every human being. The idea of physical security as one of the "natural rights" was expressed by Locke in his *Second Treatise of Government* in the sense that reason demands its recognition if men are to live together in society. Hobbes, in *Leviathan,* wrote that the instinct towards self-preservation is so strong and basic to human nature that "no law can oblige a man to abandon" it.

Situations arise in which the maintenance of an individual's right to life conflicts with his duty to abstain from violence. Legal systems generally resolve this conflict by permitting the individual's right to life to override the social duty not to use force. Where the attack or threat is sudden, the protection of society and its laws is no longer effective, and the individual alone may be left to protect his right to preserve his physical integrity on the grounds that a liberty to use force in self-defense is essential if members of society are not to be put at the mercy of the strong and unscrupulous. If a legal system is to uphold the right to life, there must be a liberty to use force for the purpose of self-defense. The corollary of this is that an attacker may, by threatening the life of another, forfeit his own right to life.

Like most matters or issues in the law, the courts face a balancing act in rendering their decisions in self-defense cases. And, again, like so many legal situations, an assessment of conflicting values must be reviewed. There always remains the danger of over-valuing the rights of an attacker or over-valuing the rights of a law-abiding citizen to preserve his physical integrity. The problems of conflicting rights and value-preferences remain concealed behind the question of "reasonableness." Decisions may therefore be taken according to the concealed assumptions of the particular judge or jury who happens to be trying the case.

A partial solution to this unacceptable state of affairs is precise legal guidelines in the statutory law among the states which have replaced the common law rules with statutory provisions. But a complete solution is not in the offering because in the final analysis ethics and values of those who render decisions will prevail. This will not always result in just outcomes, but it is the best society can do. Without the consideration of ethics and values legal principles would fail us altogether.

Appendix A
SELECTED STATE STATUTE PROVISIONS ON SELF-DEFENSE

CODE OF ALABAMA

ARTICLE 2.
JUSTIFICATION AND EXCUSE.

§ 13A-3-20. Definitions.

The following definitions are applicable to this article:

(1) FORCE. Physical action or threat against another, including confinement.

(2) DEADLY PHYSICAL FORCE. Force which, under the circumstances in which it is used, is readily capable of causing death or serious physical injury.

§ 13A-3-21. Basis for defense generally; injury to innocent person through negligence; civil remedies.

(a) *Defense.*—Except as otherwise expressly provided, justification or excuse under this article is a defense.

(b) *Danger to innocent persons.*—If a person is justified or excused in using force against a person, but he recklessly or negligently injures or creates a substantial injury to another person, the justifications afforded by this article are unavailable in a prosecution for such recklessness or negligence.

(c) *Civil remedy unimpaired.*—Any justification or excuse within the meaning of this article does not abolish or impair any civil remedy or right of action which is otherwise available. (Acts 1977, No. 607, p. 812, § 601.)

§ 13A-3-23. Use of force in defense of a person.

(a) A person is justified in using physical force upon another person in order to defend himself or a third person from what he reasonably believes to be the use or imminent use of unlawful physical force by that other person, and he may use a degree of force which he reasonably believes to be necessary for the purpose. A person may use deadly physical force if the actor reasonably believes that such other person is:

(1) Using or about to use unlawful deadly physical force; or

(2) Using or about to use physical force against an occupant of a dwelling while committing or attempting to commit a burglarly of such dwelling; or

(3) Committing or about to commit a kidnapping in any degree, assault in the first or second degree, burglarly in any degree, robbery in any degree, forcible rape or forcible sodomy.

(b) Notwithstanding the provisions of subsection (a), a person is not justified in using deadly physical force upon another person if it reasonably appears or he knows that he can avoid the necessity of using such force with complete safety:

(1) By retreating, except that the actor is not required to retreat:

    a. If he is in his dwelling or at his place of work and was not the original aggressor; or

    b. If he is a peace officer or a private person lawfully assisting a peace officer at his direction.

(2) (c) Notwithstanding the provisions of subsection (a), a person is not justified in using physical force if:

(1) With intent to cause physical injury or death to another person, he provoked the use of unlawful physical force by such other person; or

(2) He was the initial aggressor, except that his use of physical force upon another person under the circumstances is justifiable if he withdraws from the encounter and effectively communicates to the other person his intent to do so, but the latter nevertheless continues or threatens the use of unlawful physical force; or

(3) The physical force involved was the product of a combat by agreement not specifically authorized by law.

ARIZONA REVISED STATUTES

§ 13-403. Justification; use of physical force

The use of physical force upon another person which would otherwise constitute an offense is justifiable and not criminal under any of the following circumstances:

1. A parent or guardian and a teacher or other person entrusted with the care and supervision of a minor or incompetent person may use reasonable and appropriate physical force upon the minor or incompetent person when and to the extent reasonably necessary and appropriate to maintain discipline.

§ 13-404. Justification; self-defense

A. Except as provided in subsection B of this section, a person is justified in threatening or using physical force against another when and to the extent a reasonable person would believe that physical force is immediately necessary to protect himself against the other's use or attempted use of unlawful physical force.

B. The threat or use of physical force against another is not justified:

1. In response to verbal provocation alone; or

2. To resist an arrest that the person knows or should know is being made by a peace officer or by a person acting in a peace officer's presence and at his direction, whether the arrest is lawful or unlawful, unless the physical force used by the peace officer exceeds that allowed by law; or

3. If the person provoked the other's use or attempted use of unlawful physical force, unless:

    (a) The person withdraws from the encounter or clearly communicates to the other his intent to do so reasonably believing he cannot safely withdraw from the encounter; and

    (b) The other nevertheless continues or attempts to use lawful physical force against the person.

ARKANSAS STATUTES ANNOTATED

41-506. Justification—Use of physical force in defense of a person.—

(1) A person is justified in using physical force upon another person to defend himself or a third person from what he

reasonably believes to be the use or imminent use of unlawful physical force by that other person, and he may use a degree of force that he reasonably believes to be necessary. However,

(a) with purpose to cause physical injury or death to the other person, he provokes the use of unlawful physical force by the other person; or

(b) he is the initial aggressor; but his use of physical force upon another person is justifiable if he in good faith withdraws from the encounter and effectively communicates to the other person his purpose to do so, and the latter continues or threatens to continue the use of unlawful physical force; or

(c) the physical force involved is the product of a combat by agreement not authorized by law.

41-507. Justification—Use of deadly physical force in defense of a person.—

(1) A person is justified in using deadly physical force upon another person if he reasonably believes that the other person is:

(a) committing or about to commit a felony involving force or violence; or

(b) using or about to use unlawful deadly physical force.

(2) A person may not use deadly physical force in self defense if he knows that he can avoid the necessity of using that force with complete safety:

(a) by retreating, except that a person is not required to retreat if he is in his dwelling and was not the original aggressor, or if he is a law enforcement officer or a person assisting at the direction of a law enforcement officer; or

(b) by surrendering possession of property to a person claiming a lawful right thereto.

41-514. Justification—Reckless or negligent use of force— Reckless or negligent injury or risk to third parties.—

(1) When a person believes that the use of force is necessary

for any of the purposes justifying that use of force under this chapter but the person is reckless or negligent either in forming that belief or in employing an excessive degree of physical force, the justification afforded by this chapter is unavailable in a prosecution for an offense for which recklessness or negligence suffices to establish culpability.

(2) When a person is justified under this chapter in using force but he recklessly or negligently injures or creates a substantial risk of injury to a third party, the justification afforded by this chapter is unavailable in a prosecution for such recklessness or negligence toward the third party.

WEST'S ANNOTATED CALIFORNIA CODES

§ 197. Justifiable homicide; any person

Homicide is also justifiable when committed by any person, in any of the following cases:

1. When resisting any attempt to murder any person, or to commit a felony, or to do some great bodily injury upon any person; or,

2. When committed in defense of habitation, property, or person, against one who manifestly intends or endeavors, by violence or surprise, to commit a felony, or against one who manifestly intends and endeavors, in a violent, riotous or tumultuous manner, to enter the habitation of another for the purpose of offering violence to any person therein.

COLORADO REVISED STATUTES

18-1-702. Choice of evils.

(1) Unless inconsistent with other provisions of sections 18-1-703 to 18-1-707, defining justifiable use of physical force, or with some other provision of law, conduct which would otherwise constitute an offense is justifiable and not criminal when it is necessary as an emergency measure to avoid an imminent public or private injury which is about to occur by reason of a situation occasioned or developed through no conduct of the actor, and which is of sufficient gravity that, according to ordinary standards of intelligence and morality,

the desirability and urgency of avoiding the injury clearly outweigh the desirability of avoiding the injury sought to be prevented by the statute defining the offense in issue.

(2) The necessity and justifiability of conduct under subsection (1) of this section shall not rest upon considerations pertaining only to the morality and advisability of the statute, either in its general application or with respect to its application to a particular class of cases arising thereunder. When evidence relating to the defense of justification under the section is offered by the defendant, before it is submitted for the consideration of the jury, the court shall first rule as a matter of law whether the claimed facts and circumstances would, if established, constitute a justification.

18-1-704. Use of physical force in defense of a person.

(1) Except as provided in subsections (2) and (3) of this section, a person is justified in using physical force upon another person in order to defend himself or a third person from what he reasonably believes to be the use or imminent use of unlawful physical force by that other person, and he may use a degree of force which he reasonably believes to be necessary for that purpose.

(2) Deadly physical force may be used only if a person reasonably believes a lesser degree of force is inadequate and:

(a) The actor has reasonable ground to believe, and does believe, that he or another person is in imminent danger of being killed or of receiving great bodily harm; or

(b) The other person is using or reasonably appears about to use physical force against an occupant of a dwelling or business establishment while committing or attempting to commit burglary as defined in sections 18-4-202 to 18-4-204; or

(c) The other person is committing or reasonably appears about to commit kidnapping as defined in section 18-3-301, or 18-3-302, robbery as defined in section 18-4-301 or 18-4-302, sexual assault as set forth in part 4 of article 3 of title 18, or assault as defined in sections 18-3-202 and 18-3-203.

(3) Notwithstanding the provisions of subsection (1) of this section, a person is not justified in using physical force if:

(a) With intent to cause physical injury or death to another person, he provokes the use of unlawful physical force by that other person; or

(b) He is the initial aggressor, except that his use of physical force upon another person under the circumstances is justifiable if he withdraws from the encounter and effectively communicates to the other person his intent to do so, but the latter nevertheless continues or threatens the use of unlawful physical force; or

(c) The physical force involved is the product of a combat by agreement not specifically authorized by law.

3. When committed in the lawful defense of such person, or of a wife or husband, parent, child, master, mistress, or servant of such person, when there is reasonable ground to apprehend a design to commit a felony or to do some great bodily injury, and imminent danger of such design being accomplished; but such person, or the person in whose behalf the defense was made, if he was the assailant or engaged in mutual combat, must really and in good faith have endeavored to decline any further struggle before the homicide was committed; or,

4. When necessarily committed in attempting, by lawful ways and means, to apprehend any person for any felony committed, or in lawfully suppressing any riot, or in lawfully keeping and preserving the peace.

§ 198. Justifiable homicide; sufficiency of fear

BARE FEAR NOT TO JUSTIFY KILLINGS. A bare fear of the commission of any of the offenses mentioned in Subdivisions 2 and 3 of the preceding section, to prevent which homicide may be lawfully committed, is not sufficient to justify it. But the circumstances must be sufficient to excite the fears of a reasonable person, and the party killing must have acted under the influence of such fears alone.

CONNECTICUT GENERAL STATUTES ANNOTATED

§ 53a-19. Use of physical force in defense of person

(a) Except as provided in subsections (b) and (c) a person is justified in using reasonable physical force upon another person to defend himself or a third person from what he reasonably believes to be the use or imminent use of physical force, and he may use such degree of force which he reasonably believes to be necessary for such purpose; except that deadly physical force may not be used unless the actor reasonably believes that such other person is

  (1) using or about to use deadly physical force, or

  (2) inflicting or about to inflict great bodily harm.

(b) Notwithstanding the provisions of subsection (a), a person is not justified in using deadly physical force upon another person if he knows that he can avoid the necessity of using such force with complete safety

  (1) by retreating, except that the actor shall not be required to retreat if he is in his dwelling, as defined in section 53a-100, or place of work and was not the initial aggressor, or if he is a peace officer or a private person assisting such peace officer at his direction, and acting pursuant to section 53a-22, or

  (2) by surrendering possession of property to a person asserting a claim of right thereto, or

  (3) by complying with a demand that he abstain from performing an act which he is not obliged to perform.

(c) Notwithstanding the provisions of subsection (a), a person is not justified in using physical force when

  (1) with intent to cause physical injury or death to another person, he provokes the use of physical force by such other person, or

  (2) he is the initial aggressor, except that his use of physical force upon another person under such circumstances is justifiable if he withdraws from the encounter and effectively communicates to such other person his intent to do so, but such other person notwithstanding continues or threatens the use of physical force, or

  (3) the physical force involved was the product of a combat by agreement not specifically authorized by law.

DELAWARE CODE ANNOTATED

§ 463. Same—Choice of evils.

Unless inconsistent with the ensuing sections of this Criminal Code defining justifiable use of physical force, or with some other provisions of law, conduct which would otherwise constitute an offense is justifiable when it is necessary as an emergency measure to avoid an imminent public or private injury which is about to occur by reason of a situation occasioned or developed through no fault of the defendant, and which is of such gravity that, according to ordinary standards of intelligence and morality, the desirability and urgency of avoiding such injury clearly outweigh the desirability of avoiding the injury sought to be prevented by the statute defining the offense in issue. The necessity and justifiability of such conduct may not rest upon considerations pertaining only to the morality and advisability of the statute, either in its general application or with respect to its application to a particular class of cases arising thereunder.

§ 464. Same—Use of force in self-protection.

(a) The use of force upon or toward another person is justifiable when the defendant believes that such force is immediately necessary for the purpose of protecting himself against the use of unlawful force by the other person on the present occasion.

(b) Except as otherwise provided in subsections (d) and (e) of this section, a person employing protective force may estimate the necessity thereof under the circumstances as he believes them to be when the force is used, without retreating, surrendering possession, doing any other act which he has no legal duty to do or abstaining from any lawful action.

(c) The use of deadly force is justifiable under this section if the defendant believes that such force is necessary to protect himself against death, serious physical injury, kidnapping or sexual intercourse compelled by force or threat.

(d) The use of force is not justifiable under this section to resist an arrest which the defendant knows or should know is being made by a peace officer, whether or not the arrest is lawful.

(e) The use of deadly force is not justifiable under this section if:

(1) The defendant, with the purpose of causing death or serious physical injury, provoked the use of force against himself in the same encounter; or

(2) The defendant knows that he can avoid the necessity of using deadly force with complete safety by retreating, by surrendering possession of a thing to a person asserting a claim of right thereto or by complying with a demand that he abstain from performing an act which he is not legally obligated to perform except that:

> a. The defendant is not obliged to retreat in or from his dwelling; and
>
> b. The defendant is not obliged to retreat in or from his place of work, unless he was the initial aggressor; and
>
> c. A public officer justified in using force in the performance of his duties, or a person justified in using force in his assistance or a person justified in using force in making an arrest or preventing an escape, need not desist from efforts to perform the duty or make the arrest or prevent the escape because of resistance or threatened resistance by or on behalf of the person against whom the action is directed.

§ 469. Provisions generally applicable to justification.

(a) When the defendant believes that the use of force upon or toward the person of another is necessary for any of the purposes for which such relief would establish a justification under §§ 462-468 of this title but the defendant is reckless or negligent in having such belief or in acquiring or failing to acquire any knowledge or belief which is material to the justifiability of his use of force, the justification afforded by those sections is unavailable in a prosecution for an offense for which recklessness or negligence, as the case may be, suffices to establish culpability.

(b) When the defendant is justified under §§ 462-468 of this title in using force upon or toward the person of another but he recklessly or negligently injures or creates a risk of injury to innocent persons, the justification afforded by those sections is unavailable in a prosecution for an offense involving recklessness or negligence towards innocent persons.

§ 470. Definitions relating to justification.

(a) "Force," in addition to its ordinary meaning, includes confinement.

(b) "Physical force" means force used upon or directed toward the body of another person.

(c) "Unlawful force" means force which is employed without the consent of the person against whom it is directed and the employment of which constitutes an offense or actionable tort or would constitute such offense or tort except for a defense (such as the absence of intent, negligence or mental capacity; duress; youth; or diplomatic status) not amounting to a privilege to use the force. Assent constitutes consent, within the meaning of this section, whether or not it otherwise is legally effective, except assent to the infliction of death or serious bodily harm.

(d) "Deadly force" means force which the defendant uses with the purpose of causing or which he knows to create a substantial risk of causing death or serious physical injury. Purposely firing a firearm in the direction of another person or at a vehicle in which another person is believed to be constitutes deadly force. A threat to cause death or serious bodily harm, by the production of a weapon or otherwise, so long as the defendant's purpose is limited to creating an apprehension that he will use deadly force if necessary, does not constitute deadly force.

WEST'S FLORIDA STATUTES ANNOTATED

776.012 Use of force in defense of person

A person is justified in the use of force, except deadly force, against another when and to the extent that he reasonably believes that such conduct is necessary to defend himself or another against such other's imminent use of unlawful force. However, he is justified in the use of deadly force only if he reasonably believes that such force is necessary to prevent imminent death or great bodily harm to himself or another or to prevent the imminent commission of a forcible felony.

OFFICIAL CODE OF GEORGIA ANNOTATED

16-3-21. Use of force in defense of self or others.

(a) A person is justified in threatening or using force against another when and to the extent that he reasonably believes that such threat or force is necessary to defend himself or a third person against such other's imminent use of unlawful force; however, a person is justified in using force which is intended or likely to cause death or great bodily harm only if he reasonably believes that such force is necessary to prevent death or great bodily injury to himself or a third person or to prevent the commission of a forcible felony.

(b) A person is not justified in using force under the circumstances specified in subsection (a) of this Code section if he:

(1) Initially provokes the use of force against himself with the intent to use such force as an excuse to inflict bodily harm upon the assailant;

(2) Is attempting to commit, committing, or fleeing after the commission or attempted commission of a felony; or

(3) Was the aggressor or was engaged in a combat by agreement unless he withdraws from the encounter and effectively communicates to such other person his intent to do so and the other, notwithstanding, continues or threatens to continue the use of unlawful force.

(c) Any rule, regulation, or policy of any agency of the state or any ordinance, resolution, rule, regulation, or policy of any county, municipality, or other political subdivision of the state which is in conflict with this Code section shall be null, void, and of no force and effect.

16-3-23. Use of force in defense of habitation.

A person is justified in threatening or using force against another when and to the extent that he reasonably believes that such threat or force is necessary to prevent or terminate such other's unlawful entry into or attack upon a habitation; however, he is justified in the use of force which is intended or likely to cause death or great bodily harm only if:

(1) The entry is made or attempted in a violent and tumultuous manner and he reasonably believes that the entry is attempted or made for the purpose of assaulting or offering personal violence to any person dwelling or being therein and that such force is necessary to prevent the assault or offer of personal violence; or

(2) He reasonably believes that the entry is made or attempted for the purpose of committing a felony therein and such force is necessary to prevent the commission of the felony.

HAWAII REVISED STATUTES

§ 703-304 Use of force in self-protection.

(1) Subject to the provisions of this section and of section 703-308, the use of force upon or toward another person is justifiable when the actor believes that such force is immediately necessary for the purpose of protecting himself against the use of unlawful force by the other person on the present occasion.

(2) The use of deadly force is justifiable under this section if the actor believes that deadly force is necessary to protect himself against death, serious bodily injury, kidnapping, rape, or forcible sodomy.

(3) Except as otherwise provided in subsections (4) and (5) of this section, a person employing protective force may estimate the necessity thereof under the circumstances as he believes them to be when the force is used without retreating, surrendering possession, doing any other act which he has no legal duty to do, or abstaining from any lawful action.

(4) The use of force is not justifiable under this section:

(a) To resist an arrest which the actor knows is being made by a peace officer, although the arrest is unlawful; or

(b) To resist force used by the occupier or possessor of property or by another person on his behalf, where the actor knows that the person using the force is doing so under a claim of right to protect the property, except that this limitation shall not apply if:

>(i) The actor is a public officer acting in the performance of his duties or a person lawfully assisting him therein or a person making or assisting in a lawful arrest; or
>
>(ii) The actor believes that such force is necessary to protect himself against death or serious bodily injury.

(5) The use of deadly force is not justifiable under this section if:

(a) The actor, with the intent of causing death or serious bodily injury, provoked the use of force against himself in the same encounter; or

(b) The actor knows that he can avoid the necessity of using such force with complete safety by retreating or by surrendering possession of a thing to a person asserting a claim of right thereto or by complying with a demand that he abstain from any action which he has no duty to take, except that:

>(i) The actor is not obliged to retreat from his dwelling or place of work, unless he was the initial aggressor or is assailed in his place of work by another person whose place of work the actor knows it to be; and
>
>(ii) A public officer justified in using force in the performance of his duties, or a person justified in using force in his assistance or a person justified in using force in making an arrest or preventing an escape, is not obliged to desist from efforts to perform his duty, effect the arrest, or prevent the escape because of resistance or threatened resistance by or on behalf of the person against whom the action is directed.

(6) The justification afforded by this section extends to the use of confinement as protective force only if the actor takes all reasonable measures to terminate the confinement as soon as he knows that he safely can, unless the person confined has been arrested on a charge of crime.

§ 703-310. Provisions generally applicable to justification.

(1) When the actor believes that the use of force upon or toward the person of another is necessary for any of the purposes for which such belief would establish a justification under sections 703-303 to 703-309 but the actor is reckless or negligent in having such belief or in acquiring or failing to acquire any knowledge or belief which is material to the justifiability of his use of force, the justification afforded by those sections is unavailable in a prosecution for an offense for which recklessness or negligence, as the case may be, suffices to establish culpability.

(2) When the actor is justified under section 703-303 to 703-309 in using force upon or toward the person of another but he recklessly or negligently injures or creates a risk of injury to innocent persons, the justification afforded by those sections is unavailable in a prosecution for such recklessness or negligence toward innocent persons.

IDAHO CODE

§ 18-4009. Justifiable homicide by any person.

Homicide is also justifiable when committed by any person in either of the following cases:

1. When resisting any attempt to murder any person, or to commit a felony, or to do some great bodily injury upon any person; or,

. . .

3. When committed in the lawful defense of such person, or of a wife or husband, parent, child, master, mistress or servant of such person, when there is reasonable ground to apprehend a design to commit a felony or to do some great bodily injury, and imminent danger of such design being accomplished; but such person, or the person in whose behalf the defense was made, if he was the assailant or engaged in mortal combat, must really and in good faith have endeavored to decline any further struggle before the homicide was committed; or,

. . .

18-4010. Fear not sufficient justification.—

A bare fear of the commission of any of the offenses mentioned in subdivisions 2 and 3 of the preceding section, to prevent which homicide may be lawfully committed, is not sufficient to justify it. But the circumstances must be sufficient to excite the fears of a reasonable person, and the party killing must have acted under the influence of such fears alone.

19-202. Resistance by threatened party.—

Resistance sufficient to prevent the offense may be made by the party about to be injured:

1. To prevent an offense against his person, or his family, or some member thereof.
2. To prevent an illegal attempt by force to take or injure property in his lawful possession.

SMITH-HURD ILLINOIS ANNOTATED STATUTES

§ 7—1. Use of Force in Defense of Person

A person is justified in the use of force against another when and to the extent that he reasonably believes that such conduct is necessary to defend himself or another against such other's imminent use of unlawful force. However, he is justified in the use of force which is intended or likely to cause death or great bodily harm only if he reasonably believes that such force is necessary to prevent imminent death or great bodily harm to himself or another, or the commission of a forcible felony.

§ 7—4. Use of Force by Aggressor

The justification described in the preceding Sections of this Article is not available to a person who:

(a) Is attempting to commit, committing, or escaping after the commission of, a forcible felony; or

(b) Initially provokes the use of force against himself, with the intent to use such force as an excuse to inflict bodily harm upon the assailant; or

(c) Otherwise initially provokes the use of force against himself, unless:

(1) Such force is so great that he reasonably believes that he is in imminent danger of death or great bodily harm, and that he has exhausted every reasonable means to escape such danger other than the use of force which is likely to cause death or great bodily harm to the assailant; or

(2) In good faith, he withdraws from physical contact with the assailant and indicates clearly to the assailant that he desires to withdraw and terminate the use of force, but the assailant continues or resumes the use of force.

BURNS INDIANA STATUTES ANNOTATED

35-41-3-2. Use of force to protect person or property — Qualified immunity from legal jeopardy. —

(a) A person is justified in using reasonable force against another person to protect himself or a third person from what he reasonably believes to be the imminent use of unlawful force. However, a person is justified in using deadly force only if he reasonably believes that that force is necessary to prevent serious bodily injury to himself or a third person or the commission of a forcible felony. No person in this state shall be placed in legal jeopardy of any kind whatsoever for protecting himself or his family by reasonable means necessary.

(b) A person is justified in using reasonable force, including deadly force, against another person if he reasonably believes that the force is necessary to prevent or terminate the other person's unlawful entry of or attack on his dwelling or curtilage.

(c) With respect to property other than a dwelling or curtilage, a person is justified in using reasonable force against another person if he reasonably believes that the force is necessary to immediately prevent or terminate the other person's trespass on or criminal interference with property lawfully in his possession, lawfully in possession of a member of his immediate family, or belonging to a person whose property he has authority to protect. However, a person is not justified in using deadly force unless that force is justified under subsection (a) of this section.

(d) Notwithstanding subsections (a), (b), and (c) of this section, a person is not justified in using force if:

(1) He is committing, or is escaping after the commission of, a crime;

(2) He provokes unlawful action by another person, with intent to cause bodily injury to the other person; or

(3) He has entered into combat with another person or is the initial aggressor, unless he withdraws from the encounter and communicates to the other person his intent to do so and the other person nevertheless continues or threatens to continue unlawful action.

IOWA CODE ANNOTATED

704.3 Defense of self or another

A person is justified in the use of reasonable force when he or she reasonably believes that such force is necessary to defend himself or herself or another from any imminent use of unlawful force.

704.6 When defense not available

The defense of justification is not available to the following:

1. One who is participating in a forcible felony, or riot, or a duel.

2. One who initially provokes the use of force against himself or herself, with the intent to use such force as an excuse to inflict injury on the assailant.

3. One who initially provokes the use of force against himself or herself by his or her unlawful acts, unless:

  a. Such force is grossly disproportionate to the provocation, and is so great that the person reasonably believes that he or she is in imminent danger of death or serious injury or

  b. The person withdraws from physical contact with the other and indicates clearly to the other that the person desires to terminate the conflict but the other continues or resumes the use of force.

704.10 Compulsion

No act, other than an act by which one intentionally or recklessly causes physical injury to another, is a public offense if the person so acting is compelled to do so by another's threat or menace of serious injury, provided that the person reasonably believes that such injury is imminent and can be averted only by his or her doing such act.

KANSAS STATUTES ANNOTATED

21-3211. Use of force in defense of a person.

A person is justified in the use of force against an aggressor when and to the extent it appears to him and he reasonably belives that such conduct is necessary to defend himself or another against such aggressor's imminent use of unlawful force.

21-3214. Use of force by an aggressor.

The justification described in sections 21-3211, 21-3212, and 21-3213, is not available to a person who:

(1) Is attempting to commit, committing, or escaping from the commission of a forcible felony; or

(2) Initially provokes the use of force against himself or another, with intent to use such force as an excuse to inflict bodily harm upon the assailant; or

(3) Otherwise initially provokes the use of force against himself or another, unless:

(a) He has reasonable ground to believe that he is in imminent danger of death or great bodily harm, and he has exhausted every reasonable means to escape such danger other than the use of force which is likely to cause death or great bodily harm to the assailant; or

(b) In good faith, he withdraws from physical contact with the assailant and indicates clearly to the assailant that he desires to withdraw and terminate the use of force, but the assailant continues or resumes the use of force.

KENTUCKY REVISED STATUTES

503.030. Choice of evils.—

(1) Unless inconsistent with the ensuing sections of this code defining justifiable use of physical force or with some other provisions of law, conduct which would otherwise constitute an offense is justifiable when the defendant believes it to be necessary to avoid an imminent public or private injury greater than the injury which is sought to be prevented by the statute defining the offense charged, except that no justification can exist under this section for an intentional homicide.

(2) When the defendant believes that conduct which would otherwise constitute an offense is necessary for the purpose described in subsection (1), but is wanton or reckless in having such belief, or when the defendant is wanton or reckless in bringing about a situation requiring the conduct described in subsection (1), the justification afforded by this section is unavailable in a prosecution for any offense for which wantonness or recklessness, as the case may be, suffices to establish culpability.

503.050. Use of physical force in self-protection.—

(1) The use of physical force by a defendant upon another person is justifiable when the defendant believes that such force is necessary to protect himself against the use or imminent use of unlawful physical force by the other person.

(2) The use of deadly physical force by a defendant upon another person is justifiable under subsection (1) only when the defendant believes that such force is necessary to protect himself against death, serious physical injury, kidnapping, or sexual intercourse compelled by force or threat.

503.060. Improper use of physical force in self-protection.—

Notwithstanding the provisions of KRS 503.050, the use of physical force by a defendant upon another person is not justifiable when:

(1) The defendant is resisting an arrest by a peace officer,

recognized to be acting under color of official authority and using no more force than reasonably necessary to effect the arrest, although the arrest is unlawful; or

(2) The defendant, with the intention of causing death or serious physical injury to the other person, provokes the use of physical force by such other person; or

(3) The defendant was the initial aggressor, except that his use of physical force upon the other person under this circumstance is justifiable when:

(a) His initial physical force was nondeadly and the force returned by the other is such that he believes himself to be in imminent danger of death or serious physical injury; or

(b) He withdraws from the encounter and effectively communicates to the other person his intent to do so and the latter nevertheless continues or threatens the use of unlawful physical force.

LOUISIANA REVISED STATUTES

§ 19. Use of force or violence in defense

The use of force or violence upon the person of another is justifiable, when committed for the purpose of preventing a forcible offense against the person or a forcible offense or trespass against property in a person's lawful possession; provided that the force or violence used must be reasonable and apparently necessary to prevent such offense, and that this article shall not apply where the force or violence results in a homicide.

§20. Justifiable homicide

A homicide is justifiable:

(1) When committed in self-defense by one who reasonably believes that he is in imminent danger of losing his life or receiving great bodily harm and that the killing is necessary to save himself from that danger; or

(2) When committed, for the purpose of preventing a violent or forcible felony involving danger to life or of great bodily

harm, by one who reasonably believes that such an offense is about to be committed and that such action is necessary for its prevention. The circumstances must be sufficient to excite the fear of a reasonable person that there would be serious danger to his own life or person if he attempted to prevent the felony wihtout the killing.

§ 21. Aggressor cannot claim self defense

A person who is the aggressor or who brings on a difficulty cannot claim the right of self-defense unless he withdraws from the conflict in good faith and in such a manner that his adversary knows or should know that he desires to withdraw and discontinue the conflict.

MAINE REVISED STATUTES ANNOTATED

§ 108. Physical force in defense of a person

1. A person is justified in using a reasonable degree of nondeadly force upon another person in order to defend himself or a 3rd person from what he reasonably believes to be the imminent use of unlawful, nondeadly force by such other person, and he may use a degree of such force which he reasonably believes to be necessary for such purpose. However, such force is not justifiable if:

A. With a purpose to cause physical harm to another person, he provoked the use of unlawful, nondeadly force by such other person; or

B. He was the initial aggressor, unless after such aggression he withdraws from the encounter and effectively communicates to such other person his intent to do so, but the latter notwithstanding continues the use or threat of unlawful, nondeadly force; or

C. The force involved was the product of a combat by agreement not authorized by law.

2. A person is justified in using deadly force upon another person:

A. When he reasonably believes it necessary and he reasonably believes such other person is:

(1) About to use unlawful, deadly force against himself or a 3rd person; or

(2) Committing or about to commit a kidnapping, robbery or a violation of section 252, subsection 1 paragraph B, or section 253, subsection 1, paragraph A, against himself or a 3rd person; or

B. When he reasonably believes:

(1) That such other person has entered or is attempting to enter a dwelling place or has surreptitiously remained within a dwelling place without a license or privilege to do so; and

(2) That deadly force is necessary to prevent the infliction of bodily injury by such other person upon himself or a 3rd person present in the dwelling place;

C. However, a person is not justified in using deadly force as provided in paragraph A, if:

(1) With the intent to cause physical harm to another, he provokes such other person to use unlawful deadly force against anyone; or

(2) He knows that the person against whom the unlawful deadly force is directed intentionally and unlawfully provoked the use of such force; or

(3) He knows that he or a 3rd person can, with complete safety

    (a) retreat from the encounter, except that he or the 3rd person is not required to retreat if he or the 3rd person is in his dwelling place and was not the initial aggressor; or

    (b) surrender property to a person asserting a colorable claim of right thereto; or

    (c) comply with a demand that he abstain from performing an act which he is not obliged to perform.

MISSISSIPPI CODE ANNOTATED

§ 97—3—15. Homicide; justifiable homicide.

(1) The killing of a human being by the act, procurement, or omission of another shall be justifiable in the following cases:

    (e) When committed by any person in resisting any attempt unlawfully to kill such person or to commit any felony upon him, or upon or in any dwelling house in which such person shall be;

(f) When committed in the lawful defense of one's own person or any other human being, where there shall be reasonable ground to apprehend a design to commit a felony or to do some great personal injury, and there shall be imminent danger of such design being accomplished;

VERNON'S ANNOTATED MISSOURI STATUTES

563.031. Use of force in defense of persons

1. A person may, subject to the provisions of subsection 2, use physical force upon another person when and to the extent he reasonably believes such to be necessary to defend himself or a third person from what he reasonably believes to be the use or imminent use of unlawful force by such other person, unless:

(1) The actor was the initial aggressor; except that in such case his use of force is nevertheless justifiable provided

(a) He has withdrawn from the encounter and effectively communicated such withdrawal to such other person but the latter persists in continuing the incident by the use or threatened use of unlawful force; or

(b) He is a law enforcement officer and as such is an aggressor pursuant to section 563.046; or

(c) The aggression is justified under some other provision of this chapter or other provision of law;

(2) Under this circumstances as the actor reasonably believes them to be, the person whom he seeks to protect would not be justified in using such protective force.

2. A person may not use deadly force upon another person under the circumstances specified in subsection 1 unless he reasonably believes that such deadly force is necessary to protect himself or another against death, serious physical injury, rape, sodomy or kidnapping.

3. The justification afforded by this section extends to the use of physical restraint as protective force provided that the actor takes all reasonable measures to terminate the restraint as soon as it is reasonable to do so.

4. The defendant shall have the burden of injecting the issue of justification under this section.

MONTANA CODE ANNOTATED

When Force Justified

45-3-101. Definitions.

(1) "Forcible felony" means any felony which involves the use or threat of physical force or violence against any individual.

(2) "Force likely to cause death or serious bodily harm" within the meaning of this chapter includes but is not limited to:

> (a) the firing of a firearm in the direction of a person, even though no purpose exists to kill or inflict serious bodily harm; and
>
> (b) the firing of a firearm at a vehicle in which a person is riding.

45-3-102. Use of force in defense of person.

A person is justified in the use of force or threat to use force against another when and to the extent that he reasonably believes that such conduct is necessary to defend himself or another against such other's imminent use of unlawful force. However, he is justified in the use of force likely to cause death or serious bodily harm only if he reasonably believes that such force is necessary to prevent imminent death or serious bodily harm to himself or another or to prevent the commission of a forcible felony.

45-3-105. Use of force by aggressor.

The justification described in 45-3-102 through 45-3-104 is not available to a person who:

(1) is attempting to commit, committing, or escaping after the commission of a forcible felony; or

(2) purposely or knowingly provokes the use of force against himself, unless:

(a) such force is so great that he reasonably believes that he is in imminent danger of death or serious bodily harm and that he has exhausted every reasonable means to escape such danger other than the use of force which is likely to cause death or serious bodily harm to the assailant; or

(b) in good faith, he withdraws from physical contact with the assailant and indicates clearly to the assailant that he desires to withdraw and terminate the use of force but the assailant continues or resumes the use of force.

45-3-108. Use of force in resisting arrest.

A person is not authorized to use force to resist an arrest which he knows is being made either by a peace officer or by a private person summoned and directed by a peace officer to make the arrest, even if he believes that the arrest is unlawful and the arrest in fact is unlawful.

REVISED STATUTES OF NEBRASKA

28-1409. Use of force in self-protection.

(1) Subject to the provisions of this section and of section 28-1414, the use of force upon or toward another person is justifiable when the actor believes that such force is immediately necessary for the purpose of protecting himself against the use of unlawful force by such other person on the present occasion.

(2) The use of such force is not justifiable under this section to resist an arrest which the actor knows is being made by a peace officer, although the arrest is unlawful.

(3) The use of such force is not justifiable under this section to resist force used by the occupier or possessor of property or by another person on his behalf, where the actor knows that the person using the force is doing so under a claim of right to protect the property, except that this limitation shall not apply if:

(a) The actor is a public officer acting in the performance of his duties or a person lawfully assisting him therein or a person making or assisting in a lawful arrest;

(b) The actor has been unlawfully dispossessed of the property and is making a reentry or recapture justified by section 28-1411; or

(c) The actor believes that such force is necessary to protect himself against death or serious bodily harm.

(4) The use of deadly force shall not be justifiable under this section unless the actor believes that such force is necessary to protect himself against death, serious bodily harm, kidnapping or sexual intercourse compelled by force or threat, nor is it justifiable if:

(a) The actor, with the purpose of causing death or serious bodily harm, provoked the use of force against himself in the same encounter; or

(b) The actor knows that he can avoid the necessity of using such force with complete safety by retreating or by surrendering possession of a thing to a person asserting a claim of right thereto or by complying with a demand that he abstain from any action which he has no duty to take, except that:

(i) The actor shall not be obliged to retreat from his dwelling or place of work, unless he was the initial aggressor or is assailed in his place of work by another person whose place of work the actor knows it to be; and

(ii) A public officer justified in using force in the performance of his duties or a person justified in using force in his assistance or a person justified in using force in making an arrest or preventing an escape shall not be obliged to desist from efforts to perform such duty, effect such arrest or prevent such escape because of resistance or threatened resistance by or on behalf of the person against whom such action is directed.

(5) Except as required by subsections (3) and (4) of this section, a person employing protective force may estimate the necessity thereof under the circumstances as he believes them to be when the force is used, without retreating, surrendering possession, doing any other act which he has no legal duty to do, or abstaining from any lawful action.

(6) The justification afforded by this section extends to the use of confinement a protective force only if the actor takes all reasonable measures to terminate the confinement as soon as he knows that he safely can do so, unless the person confined has been arrested on a charge of crime.

NEVADA REVISED STATUTES

200.190 Justifiable and excusable homicide not punishable.

The homicide appearing to be justifiable or excusable, the person indicted shall, upon his trial, be fully acquitted and discharged.

200.200 Killing in self-defense.

If a person kill another in self-defense, it must appear that:

1. The danger was so urgent and pressing that, in order to save his own life, or to prevent his receiving great bodily harm, the killing of the other was absolutely necessary; and

2. The person killed was the assailant, or that the slayer had really, and in good faith, endeavored to decline any further struggle before the mortal blow was given.

NEW HAMPSHIRE REVISED STATUTES ANNOTATED

627:4 Physical Force in Defense of a Person.

I. A person is justified in using non-deadly force upon another person in order to defend himself or a third person from what he reasonably believes to be the imminent use of unlawful, non-deadly force by such other person, and he may use a degree of such force which he reasonably believes to be necessary for such purpose. However, such force is not justifiable if:

(a) With a purpose to cause physical harm to another person, he provoked the use of unlawful, non-deadly force by such other person; or

(b) He was the initial aggressor, unless after such aggression he withdraws from the encounter and effectively communicates to such other person his intent to do so, but the latter notwithstanding continues the use or threat of unlawful, non-deadly force; or

(c) The force involved was the product of a combat by agreement not authorized by law.

II. A person is justified in using deadly force upon another person when he reasonably believes that such other person

(a) Is about to use unlawful, deadly force against the actor or a third person, or

(b) Is likely to use any unlawful force against a person present while committing or attempting to commit a burglary, or

(c) Is committing or about to commit kidnapping or a forcible sex offense.

III. A person is not justified in using deadly force on another to defend himself or a third person from deadly force by the other if he knows that he and the third person can, with complete safety

(a) Retreat from the encounter, except that he is not required to retreat if he is in his dwelling and was not the initial aggressor; or

(b) Surrender property to a person asserting a claim of right thereto; or

(c) Comply with a demand that he abstain from performing an act which he is not obliged to perform; nor is the use of deadly force justifiable when, with the purpose of causing death or serious bodily harm, the actor has provoked the use of force against himself in the same encounter.

(d) If he is a law enforcement officer or a private person assisting him at his direction and was acting pursuant to RSA 627:5, he need not retreat.

NEW JERSEY STATUTES ANNOTATED

2C:3-4. Use of force in self-protection

a. Use force justifiable for protection of the person. Subject to the provisions of this section and of section 2C:3-9, the use of force upon or toward another person is justifiable when the actor reasonably believes that such force is immediately necessary for the purpose of protecting himself against the use of unlawful force by such other person on the present occasion.

b. Limitations on justifying necessity for use of force.

(1) The use of force is not justifiable under this section:

(a) To resist an arrest which the actor knows is being made by a peace officer in the performance of his duties, although the arrest is unlawful, unless the peace officer employs unlawful force to effect such arrest; or

(b) To resist force used by the occupier or possessor of property or by another person on his behalf, where the actor knows that the person using the force is doing so under a claim of right to protect the property, except that this limitation shall not apply if:

(i) The actor is a public officer acting in the performance of his duties or a person lawfully assisting him therein or a person making or assisting in a lawful arrest;

(ii) The actor has been unlawfully dispossessed of the property and is making a reentry or recaption justified by section 2C:3-6; or

(iii) The actor reasonably believes that such force is necessary to protect himself against death or serious bodily harm.

(2) The use of deadly force is not justifiable under this section unless the actor reasonably believes that such force is necessary to protect himself against death or serious bodily harm; nor is it justifiable if:

(a) The actor, with the purpose of causing death or serious bodily harm, provoked the use of force against himself in the same encounter; or

(b) The actor knows that he can avoid the necessity of using such force with complete safety by retreating or by surrendering possession of a thing to a person asserting a claim of right thereto or by complying with a demand that he abstain from any action which he has not duty to take, except that:

   (i) The actor is not obliged to retreat from his dwelling, unless he was the initial aggressor or is assailed in his dwelling by another person whose dwelling the actor knows it to be; and

   (ii) A public officer justified in using force in the performance of his duties or a person justified in using force in his assistance or a person justified in using force in making an arrest or preventing an escape is not obliged to desist from efforts to perform such duty, effect such arrest or prevent such escape because of resistance or threatened resistance by or on behalf of the person against whom such action is directed.

(3) Except as required by paragraphs (1) and (2) of this subsection, a person employing protective force may estimate the necessity of using force when the force is used, without retreating, surrendering possession, doing any other act which he has no legal duty to do or abstaining from any lawful action.

NEW MEXICO STATUTES ANNOTATED

30-2-7. Justifiable homicide by citizen.

Homicide is justifiable when committed by any person in any of the following cases:

A. when committed in the necessary defense of his life, his family or his property, or in necessarily defending against any unlawful action directed against himself, his wife or family;

B. when committed in the lawful defense of himself or of another and when there is a reasonable ground to believe a design exists to commit a felony or to do some great personal injury against such person or another, and there is imminent danger that the design will be accomplished; or

C. when necessarily committed in attempting, by lawful ways and means, to apprehend any person for any felony committed in his presence, or in lawfully suppressing any riot, or in necessarily and lawfully keeping and preserving the peace.

McKINNEY'S CONSOLIDATED LAWS OF NEW YORK ANNOTATED

Part 1 **JUSTIFICATION** § 35.15

§ 35.15 Justification; use of physical force in defense of a person

1. A person may, subject to the provisions of subdivision two, use physical force upon another person when and to the extent he reasonably belives such to be necessary to defend himself or a third person from what he reasonably believes to be the use or imminent use of unlawful physical force by such other person, unless:

(a) The latter's conduct was provoked by the actor himself with intent to cause physical injury to another person; or

(b) The actor was the initial aggressor; except that in such case his use of physical force is nevertheless justifiable if he has withdrawn from the encounter and effectively communicated such withdrawal to such other person but the latter persists in continuing the incident by the use or threatened imminent use of unlawful physical force; or

(c) The physical force involved is the product of a combat by agreement not specifically authorized by law.

2. A person may not use deadly physical force upon another person under circumstances specified in subdivision one unless:

(a) He reasonably believes that such other person is using or about to use deadly physical force. Even in such case, however, the actor may not use deadly physical force if he knows that he can with complete safety as to himself and others avoid the necessity of so doing by retreating; except that he is under no duty to retreat if he is:

(i) in his dwelling and not the initial aggressor; or

(ii) a peace officer or a person assisting a peace officer at the latter's direction, acting pursuant to section 35.30; or

(b) He reasonably believes that such other person is

committing or attempting to commit a kidnapping, forcible rape, forcible sodomy or robbery; or

(c) He reasonably believes that such other person is committing or attempting to commit a burglary, and the circumstances are such that the use of deadly physical force is authorized by subdivision three of section 35.20.

NORTH DAKOTA CENTURY CODE ANNOTATED

12.1-05-03. Self-defense.

A person is justified in using force upon another person to defend himself against danger of imminent unlawful bodily injury, sexual assault, or detention by such other person, except that:

1. A person is not justified in using force for the purpose of resisting arrest, execution of process, or other performance of duty by a public servant under color of law, but excessive force may be resisted.

2. A person is not justified in using force if:

   a. He intentionally provokes unlawful action by another person to cause bodily injury or death to such other person; or

   b. He has entered into a mutual combat with another person or is the initial aggressor unless he is resisting force which is clearly excessive in the circumstances. A person's use of defensive force after he withdraws from an encounter and indicates to the other person that he has done so is justified if the latter nevertheless continues or menaces unlawful action.

OKLAHOMA STATUTES ANNOTATED

§ 643. Force against another not unlawful, when—Self-defense—Defense of property

To use or to attempt to offer to use force or violence upon or toward the person of another is not unlawful in the following cases:

3. When committed either by the party about to be injured,

or by any other person in his aid or defense, in preventing or attempting to prevent an offense against his person, or any trespass or other unlawful interference with real or personal property in his lawful possession; provided the force or violence used is not more than sufficient to prevent such offense.

OREGON REVISED STATUTES

161.200 Choice of evils.

(1) Unless inconsistent with other provisions of chapter 743, Oregon Laws 1971, defining justifiable use of physical force, or with some other provision of law, conduct which would otherwise constitute an offense is justifiable and not criminal when:

(a) That conduct is necessary as an emergency measure to avoid an imminent public or private injury; and

(b) The threatened injury is of such gravity that, according to ordinary standards of intelligence and morality, the desirability and urgency of avoiding the injury clearly outweigh the desirability of avoiding the injury sought to be prevented by the statute defining the offense in issue.

(2) The necessity and justifiability of conduct under subsection (1) of this section shall not rest upon considerations pertaining only to the morality and advisability of the statute, either in its general application or with respect to its application to a particular class of cases arising thereunder. (1971 c.743 § 20]

161.205 Use of physical force generally.

The use of physical force upon another person that would otherwise constitute an offense is justifiable and not criminal under any of the following circumstances:

(1) A parent, guardian or other person entrusted with the care and supervision of a minor or an incompetent person may use reasonable physical force upon such minor or incompetent person when and to the extent the person reasonably believes it necessary to maintain discipline or to promote the welfare of

the minor or incompetent person. A teacher may use reasonable physical force upon a student when and to the extent the teacher reasonably believes it necessary to maintain order in the school or classroom or at a school activity or event, whether or not it is held on school property.

(2) An authorized official of a jail, prison or correctional facility may use physical force when and to the extent that the official reasonably believes it necessary to maintain order and discipline or as is authorized by law.

(3) A person responsible for the maintenance of order in a common carrier of passengers, or a person acting under the direction of the person, may use physical force when and to the extent that the person reasonably believes it necessary to maintain order, but the person may use deadly physical force only when the person reasonably believes it necessary to prevent death or serious physical injury.

(4) A person acting under a reasonable belief that another person is about to commit suicide or to inflict serious physical self-injury may use physical force upon that person to the extent that the person reasonably believes it necessary to thwart the result.

(5) A person may use physical force upon another in self-defense or in defending a third person, in defending property, in making an arrest or in preventing an escape, as hereafter prescribed in chapter 743, Oregon Laws 1971.

161.209 Use of physical force in defense of a person.

Except as provided in ORS 161.215 and 161.219, a person is justified in using physical force upon another person for self-defense or to defend a third person from what the person reasonably believes to be the use or imminent use of unlawful physical force, and the person may use a degree of force which the person reasonably believes to be necessary for the purpose.

161.215 Limitations on use of physical force in defense of a person.

Notwithstanding ORS 161.209, a person is not justified in using physical force upon another person if:

(1) With intent to cause physical injury or death to another person, the person provokes the use of unlawful physical force by that person;
or

(2) The person is the initial aggressor, except that the use of physical force upon another person under such circumstances is justifiable if the person withdraws from the encounter and effectively communicates to the other person the intent to do so, but the latter nevertheless continues or threatens to continue the use of unlawful physical force; or

(3) The physical force involved is the product of a combat by agreement not specifically authorized by law. [1971 c.743 § 24]

161.219 Limitations on use of deadly physical force in defense of a person.

Notwithstanding the provisions of ORS 161.209, a person is not justified in using deadly physical force upon another person unless the person reasonably believes that the other person is:

(1) Committing or attempting to commit a felony involving the use or threatened imminent use of physical force against a person; or

(2) Committing or attempting to commit a burglary in a dwelling; or

(3) Using or about to use unlawful deadly physical force against a person.

TENNESSEE CODE ANNOTATED

38-2-102. Resistance by party about to be injured.

Resistance sufficient to prevent the offense may be made by the party about to be injured:

(1) To prevent an offense against his person.

VERNON'S TEXAS CODE ANNOTATED

§ 9.31. Self-Defense

(a) Except as provided in Subsection (b) of this section, a person is justified in using force against another when and to the degree he reasonably believes the force is immediately necessary to protect himself against the other's use or attempted use of unlawful force.

(b) The use of force against another is not justified:

(1) in response to verbal provocation alone;

(2) to resist an arrest or search that the actor knows is being made by a peace officer, or by a person acting in a peace officer's presence and at his discretion, even though the arrest or search is unlawful, unless the resistance is justified under Subsection (c) of this section;

(3) if the actor consented to the exact force used or attempted by the other; or

(4) if the actor provoked the other's use or attempted use of unlawful force, unless:

(A) the actor abandons the encounter, or clearly communicates to the other his intent to do so reasonably believing he cannot safely abandon the encounter; and

(B) the other nevertheless continues or attempts to use unlawful force against the actor.

(c) The use of force to resist an arrest or search is justified:

(1) if, before the actor offers any resistance, the peace officer (or person acting at his discretion) uses or attempts to use greater force than necessary to make the arrest or search; and

(2) when and to the degree the actor reasonably believes the force is immediately necessary to protect himself against the peace officer's (or other person's) use or attempted use of greater force than necessary.

(d) The use of deadly force is not justified under this subchapter except as provided in Sections 9.32, 9.33, and 9.34 of this code.

§ 9.32. Deadly Force in Defense of Person

A person is justified in using deadly force against another:

(1) if he would be justified in using force against the other under Section 9.31 of this code;

(2) if a reasonable person in the actor's situation would not have retreated; and

(3) when and to the degree he reasonably believes the deadly

force is immediately necessary:

(A) to protect himself against the other's use or attempted use of unlawful deadly force; or

(B) to prevent the other's imminent commission of aggravated kidnapping, murder, sexual assault, aggravated sexual assault, robbery, or aggravated robbery.

REVISED CODE OF WASHINGTON ANNOTATED

Definitions.

In this chapter, unless a different meaning is plainly required:

"Necessary" means that no reasonably effective alternative to the use of force appeared to exist and that the amount of force used was reasonable to effect the lawful purpose intended.

Use of Force—When lawful.

The use, attempt, or offer to use force upon or toward the person of another is not unlawful in the following cases:

(1) Whenever necessarily used by a public officer in the performance of a legal duty, or a person assisting him and acting under his direction;

(2) Whenever necessarily used by a person arresting one who has committed a felony and delivering him to a public officer competent to receive him into custody;

(3) Whenever used by a party about to be injured, or by another lawfully aiding him, in preventing or attempting to prevent an offense against his person, or a malicious trespass, or other malicious interference with real or personal property lawfully in his possession, in case the force is not more than is necessary;

(4) Whenever reasonably used by a person to detain someone who enters or remains unlawfully in a building or on real property lawfully in the possession of such person, so long as such detention is reasonable in duration and manner to investigate the reason for the detained person's presence on the premises, and so long as the premises in question did not reasonably appear to be intended to be open to members of the public;

(5) Whenever used in a reasonable and moderate manner by a parent or his authorized agent, a guardian, master, or teacher in the exercise of lawful authority, to restrain or correct his child, ward, apprentice, or scholar;

(6) Whenever used by a carrier of passengers or his authorized agent or servant, or other person assisting them at their request in expelling from a carriage, railway car, vessel, or other vehicle, a passenger who refused to obey a lawful and reasonable regulation proscribed for the conduct of passengers, if such vehicle has first been stopped and the force used is not more than is necessary to expel the offender with reasonable regard to his personal safety;

(7) Whenever used by any person to prevent a mentally ill, mentally incompetent, or mentally disabled person from committing an act dangerous to himself or another, or in enforcing necessary restraint for the protection of his person, or his restoration to health, during such period only as is necessary to obtain legal authority for the restraint or custody of his person.

Homicide—When excusable.

Homicide is excusable when committed by accident or misfortune in doing any lawful act by lawful means, without criminal negligence, or without any unlawful intent.

Justifiable homicide by public officer.

Homicide is justifiable when committed by a public officer, or person acting under his command and in his aid, in the following cases:

(1) In obedience to the judgment of a competent court.

(2) When necessary to overcome actual resistance to the execution of the legal process, mandate, or order of a court or officer, or in the discharge of legal duty.

(3) When necessary in retaking an escaped or rescued prisoner who has been committed, arrested for, or convicted of a felony; or in arresting a person who has committed a felony and is fleeing from justice; or in attempting, by lawful ways or

means, to apprehend a person for a felony actually committed; or in lawfully suppressing a riot or preserving the peace.

Homicide—By other persons—When justifiable.

Homicide is also justifiable when committed either:

(1) In the lawful defense of the slayer, or his or her husband, wife, parent, child, brother, or sister, or of any other person in his presence or company, when there is reasonable ground to apprehend a design on the part of the person slain to commit a felony or to do some great personal injury to the slayer or to any such person, and there is imminent danger of such design being accomplished; or

(2) In the actual resistance of an attempt to commit a felony upon the slayer, in his presence, or upon or in a dwelling, or other place of abode, in which he is.

WEST'S WISCONSIN STATUTES ANNOTATED

939.48 Self-defense and defense of others

(1) A person is privileged to threaten or intentionally use force against another for the purpose of preventing or terminating what he reasonably believes to be an unlawful interference with his person by such other person. The actor may intentionally use only such force or threat thereof as he reasonably believes is necessary to prevent or terminate the interference. He may not intentionally use force which is intended or likely to cause death or great bodily harm unless he reasonably believes that such force is necessary to prevent imminent death or great bodily harm to himself.

(2) Provocation affects the privilege of self-defense as follows:

(a) A person who engages in unlawful conduct of a type likely to provoke others to attack him and thereby does provoke an attack is not entitled to claim the privilege of self-defense against such attack, except when the attack which ensues is of a type causing him to reasonably believe that he is in imminent danger of death or great bodily harm. In such a case, he is privileged to act in self-defense, but he is not privileged to resort to the use of force intended or likely to cause death to his assailant unless he reasonably believes he has exhausted every other reasonable means to escape from or otherwise avoid death or great bodily harm at the hands of his assailant.

(b) The privilege lost by provocation may be regained if the actor in good faith withdraws from the fight and gives adequate notice thereof to his assailant.

(c) A person who provokes an attack, whether by lawful or unlawful conduct, with intent to use such an attack as an excuse to cause death or great bodily harm to his assailant is not entitled to claim the privilege of self-defense.

(3) The privilege of self-defense extends not only to the intentional infliction of harm upon a real or apparent wrongdoer, but also to the unintended infliction of harm upon a third person, except that if such unintended infliction of harm amounts to the crime of injury by conduct regardless of life, injury by negligent use of weapon, homicide by reckless conduct or homicide by negligent use of vehicle or weapon, the actor is liable for whatever one of those crimes is committed.

(4) A person is privileged to defend a third person from real or apparent unlawful interference by another under the same conditions and by the same means as those under and by which he is privileged to defend himself from real or apparent unlawful intereference, provided that he reasonably believes that the facts are such that the third person would be privileged to act in self-defense and that his intervention is necessary for the protection of the third person.

(5) A person is privileged to use force against another if he reasonably believes that to use such force is necessary to prevent such person from committing suicide, but this privilege does not extend to the intentional use of force intended or likely to cause death.

(6) In this section "unlawful" means either tortious or expressly prohibited by criminal law or both.

Appendix B
AMERICAN LAW INSTITUTE MODEL PENAL CODE

Section 3.04. Use of Force in Self-Protection.

(1) *Use of Force Justifiable for Protection of the Person.* Subject to the provisions of this Section and of Section 3.09, the use of force upon or toward another person is justifiable when the actor believes that such force is immediately necessary for the purpose of protecting himself against the use of unlawful force by such other person on the present occasion.

(2) *Limitations on Justifying Necessity for Use of Force.*

    (a) The use of force is not justifiable under this Section:

        (i) to resist an arrest that the actor knows is being made by a peace officer, although the arrest is unlawful; or

        (ii) to resist force used by the occupier or possessor of property or by another person on his behalf, where the actor knows that the person using the force is doing so under a claim of right to protect the property, except that this limitation shall not apply if:

(A) the actor is a public officer acting in the performance of his duties or a person lawfully assisting him therein or a person making or assisting in a lawful arrest; or

(B) the actor has been unlawfully dispossessed of the property and is making a re-entry or recaption justified by Section 3.06; or

(C) the actor believes that such force is necessary to protect himself against death or serious bodily injury.

    (b) The use of deadly force is not justifiable under this Section unless the actor believes that such force is necessary to protect himself against death, serious bodily injury, kidnapping or sexual intercourse compelled by force or threat; nor is it justifiable if:

        (i) the actor, with the purpose of causing death or

serious bodily injury, provoked the use of force against himself in the same encounter; or

(ii) the actor knows that he can avoid the necessity of using such force with complete safety by retreating or by surrendering possession of a thing to a person asserting a claim of right thereto or by complying with a demand that he abstain from any action that he has no duty to take, except that:

(A) the actor is not obliged to retreat from his dwelling or place of work, unless he was the initial aggressor or is assailed in his place of work by another person whose place of work the actor knows it to be; and

(B) a public officer justified in using force in the performance of his duties or a person justified in using force in his assistance or a person justified in using force in making an arrest or preventing an escape is not obliged to desist from efforts to perform such duty, effect such arrest or prevent such escape because of resistance or threatened resistance by or on behalf of the person against whom such action is directed.

(c) Except as required by paragraphs (a) and (b) of this Subsection, a person employing protective force may estimate the necessity thereof under the circumstances as he believes them to be when the force is used, without retreating, surrendering possession, doing any other act that he has no legal duty to do or abtaining from any lawful action.

(3) *Use of Confinement as Protective Force.* The justification afforded by this Section extends to the use of confinement as protective force only if the actor takes all reasonable measures to terminate the confinement as soon as he knows that he safely can, unless the person confined has been arrested on a charge of crime.

* * * * * *

Section 3.09. Mistake of Law as to Unlawfulness of Force or Legality of Arrest; Reckless or Negligent Use of Otherwise Justifiable Force; Reckless or Negligent Injury or Risk of Injury to Innocent Persons.

(1) The justification afforded by Sections 3.04 to 3.07, inclusive, is unavailable when:

(a) the actor's belief in the unlawfulness of the force or conduct against which he employs protective force or his belief in the lawfulness of an arrest that he endeavors to effect by force is erroneous; and

(b) his error is due to ignorance or mistake as to the provisions of the Code, any other provision of the criminal law or the law governing the legality of an arrest or search.

(2) When the actor believes that the use of force upon or toward the person of another is necessary for any of the purposes for which such belief would establish a justification under Sections 3.03 to 3.08 but the actor is reckless or negligent in having such belief or in acquiring or failing to acquire any knowledge or belief that is material to the justifiability of his use of force, the justification afforded by those Sections is unavailable in a prosecution for an offense for which recklessness or negligence, as the case may be, suffices to establish culpability.

(3) When the actor is justified under Sections 3.03 to 3.08 in using force upon or toward the person of another but he recklessly or negligently injures or creates a risk of injury to innocent persons, the justification afforded by those Sections is unavailable in a prosecution for such recklessness or negligence towards innocent persons.

Section 3.11. Definitions.

In this Article, unless a different meaning plainly is required:

(1) "unlawful force" means force, including confinement, that is employed without the consent of the person against whom it is directed and the employment of which constitutes an offense or actionable tort or would constitute such offense or tort except for a defense (such as the absence of intent,

negligence, or mental capacity; duress; youth; or diplomatic status) not amounting to a privilege to use the force. Assent constitutes consent, within the meaning of this Section, whether or not it otherwise is legally effective, except assent to the infliction of death or serious bodily injury.

(2) "deadly force" means force that the actor uses with the purpose of causing or that he knows to create a substantial risk of causing death or serious bodily injury. Purposely firing a firearm in the direction of another person or at a vehicle in which another person is believed to be constitutes deadly force. A threat to cause death or serious bodily injury, by the production of a weapon or otherwise, so long as the actor's purpose is limited to creating an apprehension that he will use deadly force if necessary, does not constitute deadly force.

(3) "dwelling" means any building or structure, though movable or temporary, or a portion thereof, that is for the time being the actor's home or place of lodging.

Appendix C
AMERICAN LAW INSTITUTE MODEL PENAL CODE
COMMENTS

(c) *Duty to Retreat.* As has been indicated, Subsection (2)(b)(ii) denies a justification for the use of deadly force if the actor knows that he can avoid the necessity of using such force with complete safety by retreating. Exceptions are made, however, for a person attacked in his dwelling or place of work, for a public officer engaged in the performance of his duties and for a person justified in using force in making an arrest or preventing an escape.

There is a sense in which a duty to retreat may be regarded as a logical derivative of the underlying justifying principle of self-defense: belief in the necessity of the protective action. The actor who knows he can retreat with safety also knows the necessity can be avoided in that way. The logic of this position never has been accepted when moderate force is used in self-defense; here all agree that the actor may stand his ground and estimate necessity upon that basis. When the resort is to deadly force, however, Beale argued that the common law was otherwise—that the law of homicide demanded that the estimation of necessity take account of the possibility of safe retreat. Perkins challenged this conclusion in the case of actors free from fault in bringing on the struggle, urging that it was only true with respect to aggressors or cases of mutual combat. American jurisdictions, prior to approval of the Model Code, divided on the question, no less in crime than tort, with the preponderant position favoring the right to stand one's ground. In a famous opinion, Justice Holmes advanced what seems to be a median position: "Rationally the failure to retreat is a circumstance to be considered with all the others in order to determine whether the defendant went farther than he was justified in doing; not a categorical proof of guilt." This would apparently remit the issue to the jury, without a legal mandate on the point.

This issue is an old one in the deliberations of the Institute. Recognizing that it was embracing a minority position, the first Restatement of Torts affirmed a duty to avoid the necessity of using deadly force by retreating when the actor knows that he can do so with complete safety. The position has been reaffirmed in the Restatement Second. It rests, of course, upon the view that the protection of life has such a high place in a proper scheme of social values that the law should not permit conduct that places life in jeopardy, when the necessity for doing so can be avoided by the sacrifice of the much smaller value that inheres in standing up to an aggression. To the argument that retreat is cowardly and dishonorable, the answer embraced has been that of Beale: "A really honorable man, a man of truly refined and elevated feeling, would perhaps always regret the apparent cowardice of a retreat, but he would regret ten times more, after the excitement of the contest was past, the thought that he had the blood of a fellow-being on his hands." To the argument that the retreat rule cedes the field to any group of bullies prepared to make a show of deadly force, the answer has been that the proper and sufficient remedy is not a trial of strength but rather a complaint to the police. If this foregoes a private sanction that might operate as a deterrent to aggressors, it does so in reliance on the adequacy of the public sanctions and does so only when the highest value is at stake. It should, moreover, be remembered that if a privilege to stand one's ground is granted, it must extend not only to the case where the victim of protective force was actually an aggressor but also to the case where he was reasonably but erroneously thought to be.

Considerations of this sort, decisive with respect to torts, apply with equal force to penal law.

The Institute's position is thus that retreat is not required unless the actor determines that he will need to use deadly force to defend himself if he stands his ground, and even then retreat is only a requisite if the actor knows that he can avoid the need to use such *force with complete safety* by retreating. With a standard of this nature, it is to be expected that all doubts will be resolved in the actor's favor, and that such moral claim as there is to standing one's ground can easily be recognized in the doubtful cases. By the same token, however, it is clear that there is no moral claim to exoneration if the actor kills when he clearly need not do so in order to protect himself—when, in other words, he knows that he can avoid the need to kill at no risk to himself. The Code thus places a high value on the preservation of life.

Many of the recently enacted and proposed revised criminal codes in this country have taken a similar view and have included a provision on retreat in much the same terms as provided here. The Code's formulation has also influenced judicial development of the principles governing retreat.

Subsection (2)(b)(ii)(A) also follows the Restatement in adopting the traditional exception to the duty to retreat for a person who is attacked in his dwelling, a term that is defined in Section 3.11(3) of the Model Code as "any building or structure, though movable or temporary, or a portion thereof, that is for the time being the actor's home or place of lodging." Subsection (2)(b)(ii)(A) makes explicit in this context, however, that such freedom from the duty to retreat exists only for the actor who was not himself the initial aggressor.

The provision also excepts from the duty to retreat a person in his place of work. Because the sentimental factors relevant to dwellings may not apply to one's place of work, it can be argued that this extension is inappropriate; but it was concluded that the practical considerations concerning the two locations were far too similar to sustain a distinction. A second, and also difficult issue, is whether the right to stand one's ground should be preseved when the attack is by a co-dweller or co-worker. The proposal originally submitted to the Institute did not extend the exception in either instance; a wife was thus compelled to retreat from an attack by her husband in their common home (if she knew she could do so with complete safety, of course), as was one partner from an attack by another partner at their place of work. The Institute voted to require retreat from attacks at one's place of work in such a context, but not from attacks at one's dwelling. The language of Subsection (2)(b)(ii)(A) states that position.

Among those jurisdictions that have adopted a rule of retreat in recent legislative revisions, there is nearly unanimous agreement that an initial aggressor must retreat regardless of where he is threatened. There is also general agreement that one who is not an initial aggressor need not retreat from an outsider's attack within his own dwelling. Most recent revisions follow the Model Code in extending this exception to places of work, but some do not. Some require retreat if an attacker is a co-dweller or co-worker, but others do not.

There can be no controversy with respect to the exception in Subsection (2)(b)(ii)(B) for public officers justified in using force in the performance of their duties or for persons who are justified in using force in assisting such officers or in making an arrest or preventing an escape. Here, public policy demands that the function be performed and that, if forcible resistance is encountered, it be overcome. The Restatement position is unduly limited in taking account only of "an attempt to effect a lawful arrest." A person surely cannot be permitted to stultify a court order, for example, merely by threatening with death or serious injury any officer who attempts to execute it. The officer must be permitted to proceed with the performance of his duty, using such force as he believes to be essential for his own protection.

The recent revised and proposed criminal codes are in substantial agreement with the Model Code on this exception to the duty to retreat.

Appendix D
SELECTED EXCERPTS FROM OPINIONS ON SELF-DEFENSE

Tribble, convicted of manslaughter, had asserted self-defense. He was not permitted to testify about a specific act of violence he knew the victim had committed on a third person.

"Tribble sought to introduce evidence of the victim's specific act of violence against a third party, which act Tribble was aware of at time of his confrontation with Wilson. Such is not a distinction without a difference. It is only logical to conclude that when the defendant is unaware of the victim's specific acts of violence at the time of the incident such evidence sheds no light whatsoever on whether the defendant harbored a reasonable fear of imminent bodily harm at the hands of the victim. However, when the defendant is aware, at the time of the confrontation, of prior specific acts of violence committed by the victim against a third party, as in the instant case, evidence of such awareness may be highly relevant to the question of the reasonableness of the defendant's fear of imminent bodily injury at the hands of the victim." (p. 1083)

"[T]he very essence of the defense of self-defense is how the defendant perceived the situation at the time of the incident in question. We conclude, therefore, that a change in our existing rules would better serve these ends...[W]e hold that a defendant who asserts the defense of self-defense is now entitled to adduce relevant evidence of specific acts of violence perpetrated by the victim against third parties, provided however, that the defendant was aware of these acts at the time of his encounter with the victim.

"This rule, however, is not to be implemented without limitation. When it is introduced at trial, the jury should be cautioned that such evidence is only to be considered with regard to the reasonableness of the defendant's fear that the victim was about to inflict bodily harm upon him and that the evidence is not to be considered for the purpose of establishing that he probably acted in conformity, on the occasion in question, with his prior acts of violence." (p. 1085) *State v. Tribble.* 428 A.2d 1079

. . . .

"Only five years ago we were importuned, as we are again in the present case, at least in part on the basis of less restrictive holdings in other jurisdictions, to discard the rule recognized in *People v. Rodawald,* 177 N.Y. 408, 70 N.E. 1, and in self-defense cases to admit proof of specific acts of violence committed by the deceased victim for the purpose of showing that he was the aggressor. We then unanimously determined to modify the prior rule of total exclusion only to the extent, however, of holding that a trial court in the exercise of its sound discretion might 'permit a defendant in a criminal case, where justification is an issue, to introduce evidence of the victim's prior specific acts of violence of which the defendant had knowledge, provided that the acts sought to be established are reasonably related to the crime of which the defendant stands charged', if accompanied by appropriate precautionary instructions. . . We rejected the invitation to abandon the *Rodawald* rule which the dissenter would now accept. Nothing is now newly advanced by the parties or the dissenter which would warrant enlargement of the modification so recently formulated. Here, in essence, the emphasis on the particular acts of the victim as tending to show a general propensity for violence is a familiar attempt to expand inferences drawn from previous instances of behavior into proof of the actual conduct of the defendant in the circumstances of the particular crime." (pp. 391-92)

"FUCHSBERG, Judge (dissenting)."

"[M]odern codes such as the Federal Rules of Evidence, the ALI Model Code of Evidence and our own New York State Proposed Code of Evidence, not to mention the pre-eminent text writers to whom I have already referred, urge abandonment of the rule the majority would today reassert.' (p. 394) *In the Matter of Robert S.,* 42 N.E.2d 390

. . . .

"This Court has expressly stated that the test to be used when considering the affirmative defense of self-defense is 'the burden of producing sufficient evidence on the issue to raise a reasonable doubt of his guilt.' *Grady,* 166 Mont. at 175, 531 P.2d at 684 [75 NCL p. H-9]. We reaffirm that holding and hold that when a criminal defendant seeks to avail himself of the affirmative defense of the use of force in defense of another person pursuant to section 94-3-102, R.C.M. 1947, he has the burden of producing sufficient evidence on the issue to raise a reasonable doubt of his guilt." (p. 136) *State v. Cooper,* 589 P.2d 133

. . . .

"Given the inherent inconsistencies in the State's argument, we find the better construction to be that which requires that a sex offense be committed by force *in fact* before it constitutes a *'forcible sex offense'* within the meaning of section 108(2)(A)(2). Such a reading would eliminate the possibility of a person relying on those situations where the law implies force, for example, statutory rape, 17—AM.R.S.A. § 252(1)(A), but where there may not be force in fact, to invoke the defense of justification. If the above construction is applied to the case now before us, it becomes clear that the trial Justice's charge to the jury was erroneous. Defendant argued that the decedent had committed a forcible unlawful sexual contact and that he was about to commit another. The jury should have been allowed to determine if that belief was reasonable, and if so, whether the use of deadly force was necessary to repel such an attack. Affirmative responses to both questions would provide legal justification for defendant's actions." (p. 63) *State v. Philbrick,* 402 A.2d 59.

. . . .

"A person may defend himself against *any* unlawful assault. However, he is only justified in using such force as may appear to him, at the time, necessary to repel the unlawful attack. The use of force disproportionate to the necessity arising from the apprehended attack will render the person defending himself guilty of an assault. Therefore, an instruction which limits the right of self defense to only those circumstances in which the accused apprehends great bodily harm is erroneous." (p. 1231) *Degenias v. State,* 386 N.E.2d 1230

. . . .

"[W]e hold that the fact that the deceased victim had but recently discharged a gun in the course of a gambling dispute in the same premises, as two eyewitnesses would testify, and that this occurrence was known to appellant prior to the instant shooting, should have been admitted as probative of the possibility that the victim possessed a known violent character which in turn would be relevant to the appellant's alleged state of fear of serious bodily harm at the time of the shooting." (p. 971) *Commonwealth v. Stewart,* 394 A.2d 968

. . . .

"There was evidence presented at trial that defendant had just won a substantial amount of cash. The deceased repeatedly demanded some of this money, then reached for a gun and was joined by Wilson in a struggle with defendant. During the struggle Wilson reached into defendant's pocket, while defendant attempted to hold on to his money. The jury may have believed that this evidence established that defendant was resisting a robbery but used deadly force in doing so. Although this finding would have mandated an acquittal under Illinois law, the instruction to the jury did not permit such a result unless they also found that defendant was reasonably in fear of death or great bodily harm. The jury, in effect, was incorrectly instructed on the extent of the defense of justifiable use of force. This was reversible error." (p. 1311) *People v. Milton,* 390 N.E.2d 1306 (Ill.

. . . .

"We hold that appellant would have been entitled, upon proper request, to have the trial court specifically instruct the jury that the prosecution's burden of persuasion included proving that appellant had not acted in self-defense at the time of the alleged crime. However, because he failed to object at trial, appellant is not precluded from raising the failure of the court to give such an instruction as a ground for reversal on appeal, and the court's general burden of proof instruction will be deemed sufficient to cover the issue of self-defense." (p. 444) *State v. McNulty,* 588 P.2d 438

. . . .

"The fact that the deceased had a tire iron in his hands does not necessarily lead to the conclusion that he was the initial aggressor. . . . however, even if the jurors were to believe from the evidence that the decedent was the initial aggressor they could also have believed that the further actions of the defendant were proof beyond a reasonable doubt that defendant did not thereafter act in self-defense. The testimony of . . . an eyewitness . . . . was that she observed the defendant over a period of 90 seconds to two minutes; that during that time the man was walking slowly backwards and the woman walking forward, with only about a foot separating the two; that the decedent did not raise his hands which were by his side during the entire period and that she noticed the tire iron only after he fell backwards. Thus, even if the decedent were the initial aggressor, the subsequent conduct ascribed by this witness to defendant could have been viewed as without justification. While . . . . she was unable to see the deceased's hands during all of the time, it should be noted that the witness was positive that at the time the third shot was fired, the deceased's hands were at his side." (p. 1329) *People v. Adams,* 388 N.E.2d 1326

. . . .

"From a reading of the cases in this jurisdiction, our conclusion is that there has been an effort, not always successful, to reach middle ground between the two extremes, i.e., the right to stand and kill, and the duty to retreat to the wall before killing. This middle ground imposes no duty to retreat, as it recognizes that, when faced with a real or apparent threat of serious bodily harm or death itself, the average person lacks the ability to reason in a restrained manner how best to save himself and whether it is safe to retreat . . . . But this middle ground does permit the jury to consider whether a defendant, if he safely could have avoided further encounter by stepping back or walking away, was actually or apparently in imminent danger of bodily harm. In short, this rule permits the jury to determine if the defendant acted too hastily, was too quick to pull the trigger." (p. 313) *Gillis v. United States,* 400 A.2d 311

. . . .

"We hold that in a homicide prosecution where the accused has claimed self-defense, the accused may show that the deceased was the aggressor by proving the deceased's alleged character for violence. The deceased's character may be proved by reputation testimony, by opinion testimony, or by evidence of the deceased's convictions of crimes and violence, irrespective of whether the accused knew of the deceased's violent character or of the particular evidence adduced at the time of the death-dealing encounter. We emphasize that the accused is not permitted to introduce the deceased's entire criminal record into evidence in an effort to disparage his general character; only specific convictions for violent acts are admissible. Nor is the accused authorized to introduce any and all convictions of crimes involving violence, no matter how petty, how remote in time, or how dissimilar in their nature to the facts of the alleged aggression. In each case the probative value of the evidence of certain convictions rests in the sound discretion of the trial court." (p. 625) *State v. Miranda,* 405 A.2d 622

. . . .

"Simply stated, the question is whether the defense of duress as set out in A.R.S. § 13-134(5) mandates an objective test or a subjective test to determine whether the defendant felt his life was in danger. The language of the above statute appears to set up two distinct elements which the defendant must prove: (1) that he did in fact believe that his life would be endangered if he did not perform the criminal act complained of, and (2) that this belief held by the defendant was a reasonabe one. We feel that the language requiring that the defendant in fact believed that his life was endangered is placed in the statute to make it clear that the defense of duress is not available to a defendant who did not in fact believe that his life was endangered even though a reasonable man might have thought so. This reason and not a desire to mandate a subjective test was the intent of the legislature in its drafting of A.R.S. § 13-134(5). Once the defendant asserts that he was in fact in fear, his conduct is then judged by an objective standard." (p. 368) *State v. Starks,* 596 P.2d 366

. . . .

"[We] find that once there is sufficient evidence in the case to create a reasonable doubt that the killing resulted in the defendant acting in self defense, the prosecution must prove beyond a reasonable doubt that the defendant did not act in self-defense." (p. 381) *State v. Kirtley,* 252 S.E.2d 374

. . . .

"Appellant's version of the events on the day in question differ markedly from those of the State's witness. Appellant was confronted at the tennis court . . . . by Edward Mathis . . . . and Thomas Mason . . . . Mathis weighed 235 pounds and Mason weighed more. Mason was making threats to him and . . . . was carrying a tree limb and two beer bottles. Appellant fled the park on foot . . . . Ten to twenty minutes later appellant returned to the park with a shotgun to retrieve his car. When he arrived he discovered that his car, which he had left his keys in, had been locked by someone. As he approached the car, he saw Mathis crouched over in a squatting position. It appeared to appellant that Mathis was aiming something at him. Appellant explicitly testified that he thought Mathis had a gun. Appellant loaded his single barrel shotgun and fired one shot in front of Mathis to scare him. Mathis then started to move toward appellant, so he loaded a second shot and fired it in the air. . . . We find that appellant's testimony raised the issue of self-defense. Although it is questionable whether the evidence authorized a charge on provoking the difficulty, since the self-defense charge was restricted by a charge on provoking the difficulty, appellant was entitled to have the jury instructed as well on the right to carry the shotgun to the scene to protect himself against possible unlawful attack against him while he attempted to retrieve his car." (p. 363) *Williams v. State,* 580 S.W.2d 361

. . . .

"[The] testimony of the State's witnesses shows the first assault or attack was made by the appellant. The defense testimony on the other hand reflects that the appellant was attacked by both the deceased and his son before he fired the first shot. Thus, there was clear conflict in the testimony as to who made the first attack. [The] issue of provoking the difficulty does not arise from the evidence which is merely conflicting as to who made the first attack. We agree that the charge on provoking the difficulty should not have been given . . . . Even if we be wrong. . ., the court erred in failing to charge on all the elements of provoking the difficulty. The elements of provoking the difficulty—intent to provoke and act or words, or both, calculated to provoke—are still required under the 1974 Penal Code. [While] the court charged on the element of intent it failed to require the jury to find that there was an act by the appellant done with the intent to bring on the difficulty and which was reasonably calculated to bring on the difficulty. [Finally], an attempt to instruct on the converse of provoking the difficulty . . . did not instruct the jurors that if they had a reasonable doubt of whether appellant had the requisite intent or did the requisite act reasonably calculated to provoke the deceased to attack him, etc., the right of self-defense should not be forfeited." (pp. 203-04) *Dirck v. State,* 579 S.W.2d 198

. . . .

W.J.B., adjudicated a juvenile, was convicted of voluntary manslaughter after he shot and killed a paroled felon who had been terrorizing his family and 15 year old sister (because she had broken off their relationship). Watson, the felon, broke into the family home on several occasions, chased the sister, smashed doors, beat W.J.B. He broke in one night, carrying a knife, and W.J.B. shotgunned him to death. W.J.B. pled self-defense. The West Virginia Supreme Court agreed with him and modified its former positions on self-defense:

"The West Virginia cases discussing self-defense in the home are not without some confusion. While it is quite clear that we do not require the defendant to retreat before utilizing deadly force, we have been rather vague on the question of whether the occupant can use deadly force even though the intruder has not threatened the occupant with serious bodily harm or death. . .

"Despite the lack of a clear statement in our past decisions, when our cases of self-defense in the home are analyzed, it appears that we have not required the occupant to be under a reasonable apprehension of imminent danger of serious bodily harm or death in order to use deadly force on the intruder. . .

"We believe that there are sound policy reasons for permitting the homeowner to repel with deadly force a violent intrusion into his home where he has reasonable grounds to believe the intruder will commit a felony or personal injury on the occupant and that deadly force is the only means available to prevent it. First, there is still basic vitality to the ancient English rule that a man's home is his castle, and he has the right to expect some privacy and security within its confines. . .

"Second, we believe that from the standpoint of the intruder the violent and unlawful entry into a dwelling with intent to injure the occupants or commit a felony carries a common sense conclusion that he may be met with deadly force, and that his culpability matches the risk of danger. . .

"Finally, while it can be acknowleged that one element of a mature criminal justice system is to narrow the areas where individuals may resort to self-help in the infliction of punishment or the taking of life, no court has seen fit to abolish the concept of self-defense.

"In attempting to clarify our rule in regard to self-defense in the home, we do not mean to suggest that a homeowner is now free to shoot any stranger who approaches his door or that he may answer the pounding on the door with gunfire. Even an unlawful intrusion will not be sufficient when coupled only with a vague suspicion that the intruder may intend to commit a felony or physically assault the occupant. There must be a reasonable basis for the occupant's belief." (pp. 553-56) *State v. W.J.B.*, 276 S.E.2d 550

"The *uncontradicted evidence* revealed that the stabbing occurred during an argument in which the victim pursued appellant throughout the apartment, beat her, knocked her down several times, choked her, and repeatedly hit her head against the floor—all of this at a time when appellant was six months pregnant. This evidence is all that was presented at trial. At no time did appellant state that she did not think herself in danger of serious injury or death from Harvey's unprovoked attack upon her. Given these facts, we are unable to conclude beyond a reasonable doubt that appellant could not have reasonably believed that she was in danger of death or serious bodily injury." (p. 504) "The argument between appellant and Harvey occurred in appellant's home. She was therefore under no duty to leave it. Even if she had had such a duty, however, the evidence failed to establish that she could have effectuated such a retreat with safety. . . . Her statement also indicates that the kitchen had a door. Nowhere in the record, however, is there any evidence as to where that door was located relative to the sink or to the position of the parties. There is, therefore, nothing to show that appellant could have escaped through it to safety. The prosecution has thus failed to negate beyond a reasonable doubt that appellant violated any duty to retreat." (p. 505) *Commonwealth v. Helm,* 402 A.2d 500 (Pa. 5/1/79).

. . . .

"In this bizarre case, the complainant testified that defendant accompanied him to his apartment one evening; that he stripped partially so that she might massage him; that he dozed off; that he awoke, bleeding from the head and arm; that she was standing there with a meat cleaver in her hand; that he was removed to hospital, where he was treated for his wounds, undergoing brain surgery. His severe injuries were consistent with the use of a sharp, heavy instrument. The only other evidence relevant to our disposition came from defendant and the arresting detective: by defendant, that, resisting an attempt at rape by the complainant, she 'kept fighting him off' . . . 'into the kitchen' and 'picked up something heavy. . .'; the detective added that, when she surrendered at the precinct some time after the event, she told him that, 'when they were in the apartment, he came out nude and he grabbed her and she picked up an object and did it.' Neither party to the episode admitted possession of a cleaver; the instrument never was produced at the trial.

"Justification being the theme of the defense, the issue comes within the purview of Penal Law 35.15(2)(b). ['2. A person may not use deadly physical force upon another person . . . unless . . . . (b) he reasonably believe that such other person is . . . attempting to commit a . . . forcible rape. . .'] However, instead of charging pursuant to that applicable section, the court charged under subdivision (2)(a), which exculpates one who uses deadly physical force upon another in the reasonable belief 'that such other person is using or about to use deadly physical force.' There is no evidence in this case to establish a reasonable belief by defendant that the complainant intended to use deadly force on her, and, as the prosecutor candidly concedes, defendant was thereby deprived of a fair trial on her projected defense, and is entitled to trial anew on this count." (pp. 347-48) *People v. Rodriquez,* 437 N.Y.S.2d 346

. . . .

"[We] hold that a defendant may employ deadly force in self-defense *only* if it reasonably appears to be necessary to protect against death or great bodily harm. We define deadly force as force likely to cause death or great bodily harm. . . . In so holding, we expressly reject defendant's contention, and any implication in our cases in support thereof, that a defendant would be justified by the principles of self-defense in employing deadly force to protect against bodily injury or offensive physical contact. [Where] the asault being made upon defendant is insufficient to give rise to a reasonable apprehension of death or great bodily harm, then the use of deadly force by defendant to protect himself from bodily injury or offensive physical contact is excessive force as a matter of law. In cases involving assault with a deadly weapon, trial judges should, in the charge, instruct that the assault would be excused as being in self-defense only if the circumstances at the time the defendant acted were such as would create in the mind of a person of ordinary firmness a reasonable belief that such action was necessary to protect himself from death or great bodily harm. If the weapon used is a deadly weapon *per se,* no reference should be made at any point in the charge to 'bodily injury or offensive physical contact.' if the weapon used is not a deadly weapon *per se,* the trial judge should instruct the jury that if they find that defendant assaulted the victim *but do not find that he used a deadly weapon,* that assault would be excused as being in self-defense if the circumstances at the time he acted were such as would create in the mind of a person of ordinary firmness a reasonable belief that such action was necessary to protect himself from 'bodily injury or offensive physical contact'." (p. 182-4) *State v. Clay,* 256 S.E.2d 176

. . . .

"Simmons never actually made a show of deadly force toward defendant. It is this fact on which the trial court primarily relied in refusing to instruct on self-defense. Such a show of force is not, however, necessary under these circumstances. It is sufficient that defendant have a reasonable apprehension that an assault on him with deadly force is imminent. . . . Defendant claims it was his belief, as a result of the threats and the behavior to which he testified, that he was in imminent danger of great bodily harm or death. Under the evidence he presented, the reasonableness of this belief was a question for the jury. It was prejudicial error for the trial court to refuse and instruction on self-defense, and for that error defendant is entitled to a new trial." (p. 396) *State v. Spaulding,* 257 S.E.2d 391

. . . .

Appendix E

LEADING CLASSICAL U.S. SUPREME COURT DECISIONS ON THE LAW OF SELF-DEFENSE

BABE BEARD v. UNITED STATES.

ERROR TO THE CIRCUIT COURT OF THE UNITED STATES FOR THE WESTERN DISTRICT OF ARKANSAS.

No. 842. Submitted March 18, 1895. — Decided May 27, 1895.

A man assailed on his own grounds, without provocation, by a person armed with a deadly weapon and apparently seeking his life, is not obliged to retreat, but may stand his ground and defend himself with such means as are within his control; and so long as there is no intent on his part to kill his antagonist, and no purpose of doing anything beyond what is necessary to save his own life, is not guilty of murder or manslaughter if death results to his antagonist from a blow given him under such circumstances.

THE case is stated in the opinion.

Mr. John H. Rogers and *Mr. Ira D. Oglesby* for plaintiff in error.

Mr. Assistant Attorney General Dickinson for the United States.

MR. JUSTICE HARLAN delivered the opinion of the court.

The plaintiff in error, a white man and not an Indian, was indicted in the Circuit Court of the United States for the Western District of Arkansas for the crime of having killed and murdered in the Indian country, and within that District, one Will Jones, also a white person and not an Indian.

He was found guilty of manslaughter and, a motion for a new trial having been overruled, it was adjudged that he be imprisoned in Kings County Penitentiary, at Brooklyn, New York, for the term of eight years, and pay to the United States a fine of five hundred dollars.

The record contains a bill of exceptions embodying all the evidence, as well as the charge of the court to the jury, and the requests of the accused for instructions. To certain parts of the charge, and to the action of the court in refusing instructions asked by the defendant, exceptions were duly taken.

The principal question in the case arises out of those parts of the charge in which the court instructed the jury as to the principles of the law of self-defence.

There was evidence before the jury tending to establish the following facts:

An angry dispute arose between Beard and three brothers by the name of Jones—Will Jones, John Jones, and Edward Jones—in reference to a cow which a few years before that time, and just after the death of his mother, was set apart to Edward. The children being without any means for their support were distributed among their relatives, Edward being assigned to Beard, whose wife was a sister of Mrs. Jones. Beard took him into his family upon the condition that he should have the right to control him and the cow as if the lad were one of his own children, and the cow his own property. At the time Edward went to live with Beard he was only eight or nine years of age, poorly clad, and not in good physical condition.

After remaining some years with his aunt and uncle, Edward Jones left the Beard house, and determined, with the aid of his older brothers, to take the cow with him, each of them knowing that the accused objected to that being done.

The Jones brothers, one of them taking a shot-gun with him, went upon the premises of the accused for the purpose of taking the cow away, whether Beard consented or not. But they were prevented by the accused from accomplishing that object, and he warned them not to come to his place again for such a purpose, informing them that if Edward Jones was entitled to the possession of the cow, he could have it, provided his claim was successfully asserted through legal proceedings instituted by or in his behalf.

Will Jones, the oldest of the brothers, and about 20 or 21 years of age, publicly avowed his intention to get the cow away from the Beard farm or kill Beard, and of that threat the latter was informed on the day preceding that on which the fatal difficulty in question occurred.

In the afternoon of the day on which the Jones brothers were warned by Beard not again to come upon his premises for the cow unless attended by an officer of the law, and in defiance of that warning, they again went to his farm, in his absence—one of them, the deceased, being armed with a concealed deadly weapon—and attempted to take the cow away, but were prevented from doing so by Mrs. Beard, who drove it back into the lot from which it was being taken.

While the Jones brothers were on the defendant's premises in the afternoon, for the purpose of taking the cow away, Beard returned to his home from a town near by—having with him a shot-gun that he was in the habit of carrying, when absent from home—and went at once from his dwelling into the lot, called the orchard lot, a distance of about 50 or 60 yards from his house and near to that part of an adjoining field or lot where the cow was, and in which the Jones brothers and Mrs. Beard were at the time of the difficulty.

Beard ordered the Jones brothers to leave his premises. They refused to leave. Thereupon Will Jones, who was on the opposite side of the orchard fence, ten or fifteen years only from Beard, moved towards the latter with an angry manner and in a brisk walk, having his left hand (he being, as Beard knew, left-handed) in the left pocket of his trousers. When he got within five or six steps of Beard, the latter warned him to stop, but he did not do so. As he approached nearer the accused asked him what he intended to do, and he replied: "Damn you, I will show you," at the same time making a movement with his left hand as if to draw a pistol from his pocket; whereupon the accused struck him over the head with his gun and knocked him down.

"Believing," the defendant testified, "from his demonstrations just mentioned that he intended to shoot me, I struck him over the head with my gun to prevent him killing me. As soon as I struck him his brother John, who was a few steps behind him, started towards me with his hands in his pocket. Believing that he intended to take part in the difficulty and was also armed, I struck him and he stopped. I then at once jumped over the fence, caught Will Jones by the lapel of the coat, turned him rather to one side, and pulled his left hand out of his pocket. He had a pistol, which I found in his pocket, grasped in his left hand, and I pulled his pistol and his left hand out together. My purpose in doing this was to disarm him, to prevent him from shooting me, as I did not know how badly he was hurt. My gun was loaded, having ten cartridges in the magazine. I could have shot him, but did not want to kill him, believing that I could knock him down with the gun and disarm him and protect myself without shooting him. After getting his pistol, John Jones said something to me about killing him, to which I replied that I had not killed him and did not try to do so, for if I had I could have shot him. He said my gun was not loaded; thereupon I shot the gun in the air to show him that it was loaded."

Dr. Howard Hunt, a witness on behalf of the government, testified that he called to see Will Jones soon after he was hurt, and found him in a serious condition; that he died from the effects of a would given by the defendant; that the would was across the head, rather on the right side, the skull being crushed by the blow. He saw the defendant soon after dressing the wound, and told him that the deceased's condition was serious, and that he, the witness, was sorry the occurrence had happened. The witness suggested to the accused that perhaps he had better get out of the way. The latter replied that he was sorry that it had happened, but that he acted in self-defence and would not go away. Beard seemed a little offended at the suggestion that he should run off, and observed to the witness that the latter could not scare him, for he was perfetly justified in what he did. This witness further testified that he had known the defendant four or five years, was well acquainted in the neighborhood in which he lived, and knew his general reputation, which was that of a peaceable, law-abiding man.

The account we have given of the difficulty is not in harmony, in every particular, with the testimony of some of the witnesses, but it is sustained by what the accused and others testified to at the trial; so that, if the jury had found the facts to be as we have detailed them, it could not have been said that their finding was contrary to the evidence. At any rate, it was the duty of the court to tell the jury by what principles of law they should be guided, in the event they found the facts to be as stated by the accused.

Assuming then that the facts were as we have represented them to be, we are to inquire whether the court erred in its charge to the jury. In the view we take of the case, it will be necessary to refer to those parts only of the charge relating to the law of self-defence.

The court stated at considerable length the general rules that determine whether the killing of a human being is murder or manslaughter, and, among other things, said to the jury: "If these boys, or young men, or whatever you may consider them, went down there, and they were there unlawfully—if they had no right to go there—you naturally inquire whether the defendant was placed in such a situation as that he could kill for that reason. Of course, he could not. He could not kill them because they were upon his place. . . . And if these young men were there in the act of attempting the larceny of this cow and calf and the defendant killed because of that, because his mind was inflamed for the reason that they were seeking to do an act of that kind, that is manslaughter; that is all it is; there is nothing else in it; that is considered so far provocative as that it reduces the grade of the crime to manslaughter and no farther. If they had no intent to commit a larceny; if it was a bare, naked trespass; if they were there under a claim of right to get this cow, though they may not have had any right to it, but in good faith they were exercising their claim of that kind, and Will Jones was killed by the defendant for that reason, that would be murder, because you cannot kill a man for bare trespass—you cannot take his life for a bare trespass—and say the act is mitigated."

After restating the proposition that a man cannot take life because of mere fear on his part, or in order that he may prevent the commission of a bare trespass, the court proceeded: "Now, a word further upon the proposition that I have already adverted to as to what was his duty at the time. If that danger was real, coming from the hands of Will Jones, or it was apparent as coming from his hands and as affecting this defendant by some overt act at the time, was the defendant called upon to avoid that danger *by getting out of the way* of it if he could? The court says he was. The court tells you that he was. There is but one place where he need not retreat any further, where he need not go away from the danger, and that is in his dwelling-house. He may be upon his own premises, and if a man, while so situated and upon his own premises, can do that which would reasonably put aside the danger short of taking life, if he can do that, I say, he is called upon to do so by retreating, *by getting out of the way* if he can, by avoiding a conflict that may be about to come upon him, and the law says that he must do so, and *the fact that he is standing upon his own premises* away from his own dwelling-house does not take away from him the exercise of the duty of avoiding the danger if he can with a due regard to his own safety *by getting away from there* or by resorting to some other means of less violence than those resorted to. Now, the rule as applicable to a man of that kind upon his own premises, upon his own property, *but outside of his dwelling-house,* is as I have just stated." Again: "You are to bear in mind that the first proposition of the law of self-defence was that the defendant in this case was in the lawful pursuit of his business—that is to say, he was doing what he had a right to do at the time. If he was not he deprives himself of the right of self-defence, and, no matter what his adversary may do, if he by his own conduct creates certain conditions by his own wrongful conduct he cannot take advantage of such conditions created by his own wrongful act or acts. . . . Again, going to the place where the person slain is with a deadly weapon *for the purpose of provoking a difficulty or with the intent of having an affray.* Now, if a man does that, he is in the wrong, and he is cut off from the right of self-defence, no matter what his adversary may do, because the law says in the very language of these propositions relating to the law of self-defence that he must avoid taking life if he can with due regard to his own safety. Whenever he can do that he must do it; therefore, if he has an adversary and he knows that there is a bitter feeling, that there is a state of feeling that may precipitate a deadly conflict between himself and his adversary, while he has a right to pursue his usual daily avocations that are right and proper, going about his business, to go and do what is necessary to be done in that way, yet if he knows that condition I have named to exist and he goes to the place where the slain person is with a deadly weapon for the purpose of provoking a difficulty or with the intent of having an affray if it comes up, he is there to have it, and he acts for that purpose, the law says there is no self-defence for him. . . . If he went to the place where that young man was armed with a dealy weapon, even if it was upon his own premises, with the purpose of provoking a difficulty with him, in which he might use that deadly weapon, or of having a deadly affray with him, it does not make any difference what was done by the young man, there is not self-defence of the defendant. The law of self-defence does not apply to a case of that kind, because he cannot be the creator of a wrong, of a wrong state of case, and then act upon it. Now, if either one of these conditions exist, I say, the law of self defence does not apply in this case."

Later in the charge, the court recurred to the inquiry as to what the law demanded of Beard before striking the deceased with his gun, and said: "If at the time of this killing it be true that the deceased was doing an act of apparent or real deadly violence and that state of case existed, and yet that the defendant at the time could have avoided the necissity of taking his life by the exercise of any other reasonable means and he did not do that, because he did not exercise other reasonable means that would have with equal certainty saved his life, but resorted to this dernier remedy, under those facts and circumstances the law says he is guilty of manslaughter. Now, let us see what that requires. It requires, first, that the proof must show that Will Jones was doing an act of violence or about to do it, or apparently doing it or about to do it, but that it was an act that the defendant could have escaped from by doing something else other than taking the life of Jones, *by getting out of the way of that danger,* as he was called upon to do, as I have already told you, *for he could not stand there as he could stand in his own dwelling-house,* and he must have reasonably sought to avoid that danger before he took the life of Jones, and if he did not do that, if you find that to be Jones' position from this testimony, and he could have done so, but did not do it, the defendant would be guilty of manslaughter when he took the life of Jones, because in that kind of a case the law says that the conduct of Jones would be so provocative as to reduce the grade of crime; yet, at the same time, it was a state of case that the defendant could have avoided without taking his life, and because he did not do it he is guilty of the crime of manslaughter." Further: "If it be true that Will Jones at the time he was killed was exercising deadly violence, or about to do so, or apparently exercising it, or apparently about to do so, and the defendant could have paralyzed the effect of that violence without taking the life of Jones, but he did not do it, but resorted to this deadly violence when he could have protected his own life without resorting to that dernier remedy—if that be the state of case, the law says he is guilty of manslaughter, because he is doing that which he had no right to do. This great law of self-defence commands him at all times to do that which he can do under the circumstances, to wit, exercise reasonable care to avoid the danger *by getting out of the way of it,* or by exercising less violence than that which will produce death and yet will be equally effective to secure his own life. If either of these propositions exist, and they must exist to the extent I have defined to you, and the defendant took the life of Jones under these circumstances, the defendant would be guilty of manslaughter."

We are of opinion that the charger of the court to the jury was objectionable, in point of law, on several grounds.

There was no evidence tending to show that Beard went from his dwelling-house to the orchard fence *for the purpose* of provoking a difficulty, or with the *intent* of having an affray with the Jones brothers or with either of them. On the contrary, from the outset of the dispute, he evinced a purpose to avoid a difficulty or an affray. He expressed his willingness to abide by the law in respect to his right to retain the cow in his possession. He warned the Jones brothers, as he had a legal right to do, against coming upon his premises for the purpose of taking the cow away. They disregarded this warning, and determined to take the law into their own hands, whatever might be the consequences of such a course. Nevertheless, when Beard came to where they were, near the orchard fence, he did nothing to provoke a difficulty, and prior to the moment when he struck Will Jones with his gun he made no demonstration that indicated any desire whatever on his part to engage in an affray or to have an angry controversy. He only commanded the,, as he had the legal right to do, to leave his premises. He neither used, nor threatened to use, force against them.

The court several times, in its charge, raised or suggested the inquiry whether Beard was in the lawful pursuit of his business, that is, doing what he had a right to do, when, after returning home in the afternoon, he went from his dwelling-house to a part of his premises near the orchard fence, just outside of which his wife and the Jones brothers were engaged in a dispute—the former endeavoring to prevent the cow from being taken away, the latter trying to drive it off the premises. Was he not doing what he had the legal right to do, when, keeping within his own premises and near his dwelling, he joined his wife who was in dispute with others, one of whom, as he had been informed, had already threatened to take to cow away or kill him? We have no hesitation in answering this question in the affirmative.

The court also said: "The use of provoking language, or, it seems, resorting to any other device in order to get another to commence an assault so as to have a pretext for taking his life, agreeing with another to fight him with a deadly weapon, either one of these cases, if they exist as the facts in this case, puts the case in such an attitude that there is no self-defence in it." We are at a loss to understand why any such hypothetical cases were put before the jury. The jury must have supposed that, in the opinion of the court, there was evidence showing that Beard sought an opportunity to do physical harm to the Jones boys, or to some one of them. There was not the slightest foundation in the evidence for the intimation that Beard had used provoking language or resorted to any device in order to have a pretext to take the life of either of the brothers. Much less was there any reason to believe that there was an agreement to fight with deadly weapons.

But the court below committed an error of a more serious character when it told the jury, as in effect it did by different forms of expression, that if the accused could have saved his own life and avoided taking the life of Will Jones by retreating from and getting out of the way of the latter as he advanced upon him, the law makde it his duty to do so; and if he did not, when it was in his power to do so without putting his own life or boy in imminent peril, he was guilty of manslaughter. The court seemed to think if the deceased had advanced upon the accused while the latter was in his dwelling-house and under such circumstances as indicated the intention of the former to take life or inflict great bodily injury, and if, without retreating, the accused had taken the life of his assailant, having at the time reasonable grounds to believe, and in good faith believing, that his own life would be taken or great bodily harm done him unless he killed the accused, the case would have been one of justifiable homicide. To that proposition we give our entire assent. But we cannot agree that the accused was under any greater obligation, when on his own premises, near his dwelling-house, to retreat or run away from his assailant, than he would have been if attacked within his dwelling-house. The accused being where he had a right to be, on his own premises, constituting a part of his residence and home, at the time the deceased approached him in a threatening manner, and not having by language or by conduct provoked the deceased to assault him, the question for the jury was whether, without fleeing from his adversary, he had, at the moment he struck the deceased, reasonable grounds to believe, and in good faith believed, that he could not save his life or protect himself from great bodily harm except by doing what he did, namely strike the deceased with his gun, and thus prevent his further advance upon him. Even if the jury had been prepared to answer this question in the affirmative—and if it had been so answered the defendant should have been acquitted—they were instructed that the accused could not properly be acquitted on the ground of self-defence if they believed that, by retreating from his adversary, by "getting out of the way," he could have avoided taking life. We cannot give our assent to this doctrine.

The application of the doctrine of "retreating to the wall" was carefully examined by the Supreme Court of Ohio in *Erwin* v. *State,* 29 Ohio St. 186, 193, 199. That was an indictment for murder, the defendant being found guilty. The trial court charged the jury that if the defendant was in the lawful pursuit of his business at the time the fatal shot was fired, and was attacked by the deceased under circumstances denoting an intention to take life or to do great bodily harm, he could lawfully kill his assailant provided he used all means *"in his power"* otherwise to save his own life or prevent the intended harm, "such as retreating as far as he can, or disabling his adversary, without killing him, *if it be in his power;*" that if the attack was so sudden, fierce, and violent that a retreat would not diminish but increase the defendant's danger, he might kill his adversary without retreating; and further, that if from the character of the attack there was reasonable ground for defendant to believe, and he did honestly believe, that his life was about to be taken, or he was to suffer great bodily harm, and that he believed honestly that he would be in equal danger by retreating, then, if he took the life of the assailant, he was excused. Of this charge the accused complained.

Upon a full review of the authorities and looking to the principles of the common law, as expounded by writers and courts of high authority, the Supreme Court of Ohio held that the charge was erroneous, saying: "It is true that all authorities agree that the taking of life in defence of one's person cannot be either justified or excused, except on the ground of *necessity;* and that such necessity must be imminent at the time; and they also agree that no man can avail himself of such necessity if he brings it upon himself. The question then is simply this: Does the law hold a man who is violently and feloniously assaulted responsible for having brought such necessity upon himself on the sole ground that he failed to fly from his assailant when he might safely have done so? The law, out of tenderness for human life and the frailties of human nature, will not permit the taking of it to repel a mere trespass, or even to save life where the assault is provoked; but a true man who is without fault is not obliged to fly from an assailant, who by violence or surprise maliciously seeks to take his life or do him enormous bodily harm. Now, under the charge below, notwithstanding the defendant may have been without fault, and so assaulted, with the necessity of taking life to save his own upon him; still the jury could not have acquitted if they found he had failed to do all in his power otherwise to save his own life, or prevent the intended harm, as retreating as far as he could, etc. In this case we thing the law was not correctly stated."

In *Runyan* v.*State,* 57 Indiana, 80, 84, which was an indictment for murder, and where the instructions of the trial court involved the present question, the court said: "A very brief examination of the American authorities makes it evident that the ancient doctrine, as to the duty of a person assailed to retreat as far as he can, before he is justified in repelling force by force, has been greatly modified in this country, and has with us a much narrower application than formerly. Indeed, the tendency of the American mind seems to be very strongly against the enforcement of any rule which requires a person to flee when assailed, to avoid chastisement or even to save human life, and that tendency is well illustrated by the recent decisions of our courts, bearing on the general subject of the right of self-defence. The weight of modern authority, in our judgment, establishes the doctrine that, when a person, being without fault and in a place where he has a right to be, is violently assaulted, he may, without retreating, repel force by force, and if, in the reasonable exercise of his right of self-defence, his assailant is killed, he is justifiable. . . . It seems to us that the real question in the case, when it was given to the jury, was, was the defendant, under all the circumstances, justified in the use of a deadly weapon in repelling the assault of the deceased? We mean by this, did the defendant have reason to believe, and did he in fact believe, that what he did was necessary for the safety of his own life or to protect him from great bodily harm? On that question the law is imple and easy of solution, as has been already seen from the authorities cited above."

In East's Pleas of the Crown, the author, considering what sort of an attack it was lawful and justifiable to resist, even by the death of the assailant, says: "A man may repel force by force, in defence of his person, habitation or property, against one who manifestly intends or endeavors, *by violence or surprise,* to commit a know felony, such as murder, rape, robbry, arson, burglary, and the like, upon either. In these cases he is not obliged *to retreat,* but may pursue his adversary until he has secured himself from all danger; and if he kill him in so doing it is called justifiable self-defence; as, on the other hand, the killing by such felon of any person so lawfully defending himself will be murder. But a bare fear of any of these offences, however well grounded, as that another lies in wait to take away the party's life, unaccompanied with any overt act indicative of such an intention, will not warrant in killing that other by way of prevention. There must be an actual danger at the time." p. 271. So in Foster's Crown Cases: "In the case of justifiable self defence, the injured party may repel force with force in defence of his person, habitation, or property, against one who manifestly intendeth and endeavoreth, with violence or surprise, to commit a known felony upon either. In these cases he is not obliged to retreat, but may pursue his adversary till he findeth himself out of danger, and if, in a conflict between them, he happeneth to kill, such killing is justifiable." c. 3, p. 273.

In Bishop's New Crimnal Law, the author, after observing that cases of mere assault, and of mutual quarrel, where the attacking party has not the purpose of murder in his heart, are those to which is applied the doctrine of the books, that one cannot justify the killing of another, though apparently in self-defence, unless he retreat to the wall or other interposing obstacle before resorting to this extreme right, says that "where an attack is made with murderous intent, the person attacked is under no duty to fly; he may stand his ground, and if need be, kill his adversary. *And it is the same where the attack is with a deadly weapon,* for in this case the person attacked may well assume that the other intends murder, whether he does in fact or not." Vol. 1, § 850. The rule is thus expressed by Wharton: "A man may repel force by force in the defence of his person, habitation, or property, against any one or many who manifestly intent and endeavor by violence or surprise to commit a known felony on either. In such case he is not compelled to retreat, but may pursue his adversary until he finds himself out of danger, and if in the conflict between them he happen to kill him, such killing is justifiable." 2 Wharton on Crim. Law, § 1019, 7th rev. ed. Phila. 1874. See also *Gallagher* v. *State,* 3 Minnesota, 270, 273; *Pond* v. *People,* 8 Michigan, 150, 177; *State* v. *Dixon,* 75 N. C. 275, 295; *State* v. *Sherman,* 16 R. I. 631; *Fields* v. *State,* 32 N. E. Rep. 780; *Eversole* v. *Commonwealth,* 26 S. W. Rep. 816; *Haynes* v. *State,* 17 Georgia, 465, 483; *Long* v. *State,* 52 Mississippi, 23, 35; *Tweedy* v. *State,* 5 Iowa, 433; *Baker* v. *Commonwealth,* 19 S. W. Rep. 975; *Tingle* v. *Commonwealth,* 11 S. W. 812; 3 Rice's Ev. § 360.

In our opinion, the court below erred in holding that the accused, while on his premises, outside of his dwelling-house, was under a legal duty to get out of the way, if he could, of his assailant, who, according to one view of the evidence, had threatened to kill the defendant, in execution of that purpose had armed himself with a deadly weapon, with that weapon concealed upon his person went to the defendant's premises, despite the warning of the latter to keep away, and by word and act indicated his purpose to attack the accused. The defendant was where he had the right to be, when the deceased advanced upon him in a threatening manner, and with a deadly weapon; and if the accused did not provoke the assault and had at the time reasonable grounds to believe and in good faith believed, that the deceased intended to take his life or do him great bodily harm, he was not obliged to retreat, nor to consider whether he could safely retreat, but was entitled to stand his ground and meet any attack made upon him with a deadly weapon, in such way and with such force as, under all the circumstances, he, at the moment, honestly believed, and had reasonable grounds to believe, was necessary to save his own life or to protect himself from great bodily injury.

As the proceedings below were not conducted in accordance with these principles, the judgment must be reversed and the cause remanded with directions to grant a new trial.

Other objections to the charge of the court are raised by the assignments of error, but as the questions which they present may not arise upon another trial, they will not be now examined.

Judgment reversed.

ROWE v. UNITED STATES.

ERROR TO THE CIRCUIT COURT OF THE UNITED STATES FOR THE WESTERN DISTRICT OF ARKANSAS.

No. 439. Submitted October 22, 1896. — Decided November 30, 1896.

Statement of the Case.

THIS was an indictment for murder, alleged to have been committed by the plaintiff in error, in the Cherokee Nation, Indian Territory, on the 30th day of March, 1895,—the person killed, Frank Bozeman, being a white man and not an Indian. The verdict was guilty of manslaughter, and a motion for new trial having been overruled, the accused was sentenced to imprisonment in the penitentiary at Columbus, Ohio, for the term of five years, and to pay to the United States a fine of five hundred dollars.

The following agreed statement as to the evidence is taken from the record:

"The testimony on the part of the government tended to show that on the evening of the 30th of March, 1895, the defendant, David Cul Rowe, who is a Cherokee Indian, and the deceased, Frank Bozeman, a white man, a citizen of the United States, and not an Indian, met at a hotel at Pryor's Creek, Indian Territory, at the supper table; that the defendant appeared to be drinking, but was not much intoxicated; that defendant said that he has his gun, and that he had a right to carry it, as he was a 'traveller'; that he had made a gun play in that town on one occasion and he would make another one; that he said to deceased, 'What do you think of that?' The deceased did not reply, and defendant said to him, 'God damn you, I'll make you hide out or I'll make you talk to me'; that in a short time deceased got though his supper and walked out into the office of the hotel, and presently defendant came out of the dining-room; that defendant said something to deceased, which was not understook by the witnesses, but the deceased did not answer; that defendant turned to some other parties present and said, 'He (meaning deceased) will not talke to me';

that one of the parties addressed said to defendant, 'Talk Cherokee to him'; that the deceased then said, 'He has got too damn much nigger blood in him to talk anything with any sense'; that defendant then kicked at deceased, hitting him lightly on the lower part of the leg; that immediately deceased sprang at defendant, striking him with a knife and cutting him in two places in the face; that after deceased began cutting defendant the latter drew his pistol and fired, shooting deceased through the body; that at the time the defendant fired the two men were in striking distance of one another. The shot struck deceased in the right arm, near the elbow, and ranged through the body from right to left sid; that when shot was fired deceased ran, and when defendant turned round the blood was streaming from his face, where he had been cut by deceased, and he said to the bystanders to go for a doctor, that he was killed; that a short time after the difficulty the knife used by deceased on defendant was found near the place where the trouble occurred; that a knife was also found on the person of deceased after his death.

"The testimony on the part of the defence tended to who that on the day of the difficulty defendant came into town from his home, about twenty miles distant, with his wife to do some shopping; that he brought his pistol with him and left it at the livery stable where he put up his team, and at supper time went by the stable and got his pistol, fearing that it might be stolen; that defendant di not have anything to say to deceased in the dining-room, but was talking with the father of the deceased, and that defendant was not intoxicated; that when defendant came out in the office deceased used the language indicated in the statement for the government, or words to that effect, and defendant kicked at him and probably struck him lightly; that when defendant kicked he stepped back and leaned up against the counter and deceased sprang at him and began cutting him with a knife; that deceased cut him in the face and kept on striking at him with the knife, and after he was cut in the face defendant drew his pistol and fired at deceased, who was in the act of striking him again with the knife. The foregoing is in substance the statement of the defendant who testified in his own behalf.

"Proof was also offered tending to show that the reputation of the deceased as a dangerous and lawless man was bad; that the reputation of the defendant as a peaceable and law-abiding man was good, and that the reputation of prosecuting witness Thomas Boseman was bad for truth in the communities where he had resided."

The court delivered an oral charge, occupying twenty-seven pages of the printed record, and embracing a discussion of most of the leading principles in criminal law, as well as many extracts from adjudged cases and elementary treatises.

Referring to the law of self-defence, the court said to the jury:

"A man might be to some extent in the wrong, and yet he might avail himself of the law of self-defence, but what is meant by his being in the lawful pursuit of his business means that he is not himself attempting to kill, or that he is not doing an act which may directly and immediately produce a deadly affray between himself and his adversary. He is not allowed to do either. The only time when he can do an act of that kind is when the condition exists which gives him the right to invoke this law. I say if he is attempting directly to kill, he is not in the lawful pursuit of his business unless it is in his own defence under this law; and when he is doing a wrongful act which immediately contributes to the result—brings into existence an affray in which violence may be used by the adversary and he may kill because of that violence—when that is the case, the law says he is so far the author of that violent condition as that he cannot invoke this law of self-defence, and it depends upon the circumstances and conditions of the case whether or not he can invoke the law so far as to have his crime mitigated from murder to manslaughter. Then, when he is in the lawful pursuit of his business—that is, when he is occupying the relation to the state of case where the killing occurred which I have named—and then is attakced by another under circumstances which denote an intention to take away his life or to do him some enormous bodily harm, he may lawfully kill the assailant, provided he use all the means in his power otherwise to save his own life or prevent the intended harm, such as retreating as far as he can or disabling his adversary without killing him, if it be in his power. Now, let us go over that again and see what these propositions are. He must be measurably in the right—and I have defined to you what that means—and when he is so situated he is attacked, in this case, by Frank Bozeman, the man who was killed, and attacked under circumstances which denoted an intention to take away the life or to do him some enormous bodily harm, he may lawfully kill the assailant, provided he use all the means in his power otherwise to save his own life or prevent the intended harm, such s retreating as far as he can or disabling his adversary without killing him, if it be in his power. This proposition implies that he is measurably in the right. If he is doing any of these things which I will give you after awhile, which deprive him of the law of self-defence because of his own conduct in precipitating a conflict in which he kills, then he is not in the right; he is not doing what he had a right to do, and this proposition of the law of self-defence would not avail him; he could not resort to it, because his own conduct puts him in an attitude where, in the eye of the law, he is by his own wrong the creator of the necessity under which he acts, and he cannot invoke that necessity. The necessity must be one created by the man slain and which was not brought into existence by the direct act of the defendant contributing to that necessity."

After saying that both the accused and the deceased were upon the same plane in respect of the place or house in which they were at the time, each having the right to be there, the court proceeded: "Neither one of them was required to retreat under such circumcstances, because the hotel or temporary stopping place of a man may be regarded as his dwelling place, and the law of retreat in a case like that is different from what it would be on the outside. Still, situated as was the defendant and as was the deceased, there was a rule incumbent upon both of them which required that they should use all reasonable means to avoid the condition which led to a deadly conflict, whether that means could have been avoided by keeping out of the affray or by not going into it or by stepping to one side; and this law says again that if a man is in the right, if he stands without being the creator of that condition and that condition is created by the man whom he kills, and the man is doing that in the shape of exercising an act of violence which may destroy his life or inflict great injury upon his person, yet if he could have paralyzed that arm, if he could have turned aside that danger by an act of less deadly character than the one he did exercise, the law says he must do that. If he could have inflicted a less dangerous wound upon the man under the circumstances the law commands him to do that, because when he is doing that he is accomplishing the only purpose the law of self-defence contemplates he has right to accomplish—that is, to protect himself and not to execute vengeance, not to recklessly, wantonly and wickedly destroy human life, but to protect his own life when he is in the right and the other party is in the wrong."

MR. JUSTICE HARLAN, after stating the case as above reported, delivered the opinion of the court.

We think that these portions of the charge (to which the accused duly excepted) were well calculated to mislead the jury. They expressed an erroneous view of the law of self-defence. The duty of the jury was to consider the case in the light of all the facts. The evidence on behalf of the government tended to show that the accused sought a difficulty with some one; that on behalf of the accused, would not justify any such conclusion, but rather that he had the reputation of being a peaceable and law-abiding man. But the evidence on both sides was to the effect that the deceased used language of an offensive character for the purpose of provoking a difficulty with the accused, or of subjecting him to the indignity of a personal insult. The offensive words did not, it is true, legally justify the accused in what he did—the evidence of the government tending to show that "he kicked at deceased, hitting him lightly on the lower part of the leg"; that on the part of the accused tending nto show that he "kicked at" the deceased and "probably struck him lightly." According to the evidence of the defence, the accused then "stepped back, and leaned up against the counter," indicating thereby, it may be, that he neither desired nor intended to pursue the matter further. If the jury believed the evidence on behalf of the defence, they might reasonably have inferred from the actions of the accused that he did not intend to make a violent or dangerous personal assault upon the deceased, but only, by kicking at him or kicking him lightly, to express his indignation at the offensive language of the deceased. It should have been submitted to the jury whether the act of the accused in stepping back and leaning against the counter, not in an attitude for personal conflict, was intended to be, and should have been reasonably interpreted as being, a withdrawal by the accused in good faith from further controversy with the deceased. On the contrary, the court, in effect, said that if, because of words used by the deceased, the accused kicked the deceased, however lightly, and no matter how offensive those words were, he put himself in a position to make the killing manslaughter, even if the taking of life became, by reason of the suddenness, rapidity and fierceness of the assault of the deceased, absolutely necessary to save his own. By numerous quotations from adjudged cases, the court, by every form of expression, pressed upon the jury the proposition that "a person who has slain another cannot urge in justification of the killing a necessity produced by his own unlawful and wrongful acts." But that abstract principle has no application to this case, if it be true—as the evidence on behalf of the defence tended to show—that the first real provocation came from the deceased when he used towards the accused immediately after kicking at or lightly kicking the deceased, signified by his conduct that he no longer desired controversy with his adversary; whereupon the deceased, despite the efforts of the accused to retire from further contest, sprang at the latter, with knife in hand, for the purpose of taking life, and would most probably have accomplished that object, if the accused had not fired at the moment he did. Under such circumstances, did the law require that the accused should stand still, and permit himself to be cut to pieces, under the penalty that if he met the unlawful attack upon him and saved his own life, by taking that of his assailant, he would be guilty of manslaughter? We think not.

If a person, under the provacation of offensive language, assaults the speaker personally, but in such a way as to show that there is no intention to do him serious bodily harm, and then retires under such circumstances as show that he does not intend to do anything more, but in good faith withdraws from further contest, his right of self-defence is restored when the person assaulted, in violation of law, pursues him with a deadly weapon and seeks to take his life or do him great bodily harm. In *Parker* v. *The State,* 88 Alabama, 4, 7, the court, after advertising to the general rule that the aggressor cannot be heard to urge in his justification a necessity for the killing which was produced by his own wrongful act, said: "The rule, however, is not of absolute and universal application. An exception to it exists in cases where, although the defendant originally provoked the conflict, he withdraws from it in good faith, and clearly announces his desire for peace. If he be pursued after this, his right of self-defence, though once lost, revives. 'Of course,' says Mr. Wharton, in referring to this modification of the rule, 'there must be a real and *bona fide* surrender and withdrawal on his part; for, if there be not, then he will continue to be regarded as the aggressor.' 1 Wharton's Cr. Law, (9th ed.) § 486. The meaning of the principle is that the law will always leave the original aggressor an opportunity to repend before he takes the life of his adversary. Bishop's Cr. Law, (7th ed.) § 871." Recognizing this exception to be a just one, the court properly said, in addition: "Due caution must be observed by courts and juries in its application, as it involves a principle which is very liable to abuse. The question of the good or bad faith of the retreating party is of the utmost importance, and should generally be submitted to the jury in connection with the fact of retreat itself, especially where there is any room for conflicting inferences on this point from the evidence." Both parties to a mutual combat are wrong-doers, and the law of self-defence cannot be invoked by either, so long as he continues in the combat. But, as said by the Supreme Court of Iowa in *State* v. *Dillon,* 74 Iowa, 653, 659, if one "actually and in good faith withdraws from the combat, he ceases to be a wrong-doer; and if his adversary have reasonable ground for holding that he has so withdrawn, it is sufficient, even though the fact is not clearly evinced." See also 1 Bishop's New Crim. Law, § 702; *People* v. *Robertson,* 67 California, 646, 650; *Stoffer's case,* 15 Ohio St. 47. In Wharton on Homicide, § 483, the author says that "though the defendant may have thus provoked the conflict, yet, if he withdrew from it in good faith and clearly announced his desire for peace, then, if he be pursued, his rights of self-defence revive."

We do not mean to say that the jury ought to have found that the accused, after kicking the deceased lightly, withdrew in good faith from further contest and that his conduct should have been so interpreted. It was for the jury to say whether the withdrawal was in good faith, or was a mere device by the accused to obtain some advantage of his adversary. But we are of opinion that, under the circumtances, they might have found that the accused, although in the wrong when he kicked or kicked at the deceased, did not provoke the fierce attack made upon him by the latter, with knife in hand, in any sense that would deprive him altogether of the right of self-defence against such attack. If the accused did, in fact, withdraw from the combat, and intended so to do, and if his conduct should have been reasonably so interpreted by the deceased, then the assault of the latter with a deadly weapon, with the intent to take the life of the accused or to do him great bodily harm, entitled the latter to the benefit of the principle announced in *Beard* v. *United States,* 158 U.S. 550, 564, in which case it was said: "The defendant was where he had a right to be when the deceased advanced upon him in a threatening manner and with a deadly weapon; and if the accused did not provoke the assault, and had at the time reasonable grounds to believe, and in good faith believed, that the deceased intended to take his life or to do him great bodily harm, he was not obligated to retreat, nor to consider whether he could safely retreat, but was entitled to stand his ground and meet any attack made upon him with a deadly weapon, in such a way and with such force as, under all the circumstances, he, at the moment, honestly believed, and had reasonable grounds to believe, was necessary to save his own life or to protect himself from great bodily injury."

The charge, as above quoted, is liable to other objections. The court said that both the accused and the deceased had a right to be in the hotel, and that the law of retreat in a case like that is different from what it would be if they had been on the outside. Still, the court said that, under the circumstances, both parties were under a duty to use all reasonable means to avoid a collision that would lead to a deadly conflict, such as keeping out of the affray, or by not going into it, or "by stepping to one side"; and if the accused could have saved his life, or protected himself against great bodily harm, by inflicting a less dangerous wound than he did upon his assailant, or "if he could have paralyzed that arm," without doing more serious injury, the law commanded him to do so. In other words, according to the theory of the charge, although the deceased sprang at the accused, with knife in hand, for the purpose of cutting him to pieces, yet if the accused could have stepped aside or paralyzed the arm of his assailant, his killing the latter was not in the exercise of the right of self-defense. The accused was where he had the right to be, and the law did not require him to step aside when his assailant was rapidly advancing upon him with a deadly weapon. The danger in which the accused was, or believed himself to be, at the moment he fired is to some extent indicated by the fact, proved by the government, that immediately after he disabled his assailant (who had two knives upon his person) he said that he, the accused, was himself mortally wounded and wished a physician to be called. The accused was entitled, so far as his right to resist the attack was concerned, to remain where he was, and to do whatever was necessary or what he had reasonable grounds to believe at the time was necessary, to save his life or to protect himself from great bodily harm. And under the circumstances, it was error to make the case depend in whole or in part upon the inquiry whether the accused could, by stepping aside, have avoided the attack, or could have so carefully aimed his pistol as to paralyze the arm of his assailant without more seriously wounding him.

Without referring to other errors alleged to have been committed, the judgment below is reversed and the case is remanded for a new trial.

Reversed.

MR. JUSTICE BROWN and MR. JUSTICE PECKHAM dissented.

BROWN v. UNITED STATES.

CERTIORARI TO THE CIRCUIT COURT OF APPEALS FOR THE FIFTH CIRCUIT.

No. 103. Argued November 19, 1920. — Decided May 16, 1921.

MR. JUSTICE HOLMES delivered the opinion of the court.

The petitioner was convicted of murder in the second degree committed upon one Hermes at a place in Texas within the exclusive jurisdiction of the United States, and the judgment was affirmed by the Circuit Court of Appeals. 257 Fed. Rep. 46. A writ of certiorari was granted by this Court. 250 U.S. 637. Two questions are raised. The first is whether the indictment is sufficient, inasmuch as it does not allege that the place of the homicide was acquired by the United States "for the erection of a fort, magazine, arsenal, dock-yard, or other needful building," although it does allege that it was acquired from the State of Texas by the United States for the exclusive use of the United States for its public purposes and was under the exclusive jurisdiction of the same. Penal Code of March 4, 1909, c. 321, § 272, Third. 35 Stat. 1088. Constitution, Art I, § 8. In view of our opinion upon the second point we think it unnecessary to do more than to refer to the discussion in the Court below upon this.

The other question concerns the instructions at the trial. There had been trouble between Hermes and the defendant for a long time. There was evidence that Hermes had twice assaulted the defendant with a knife and had made threats communicated to the defendant that the next time, one of them would go off in a black box. On the day in question the defendant was at the place above mentioned superintending excavation work for a postoffice. In view of Herme's threats he had taken a pistol with him and had laid it in his coat upon a dump. Hermes was driven up by a witness, in a cart to be loaded, and the defendant said that certain earth was not to be removed, whereupon Hermes came toward him, the defendant says, with a knife. The defendant retreated some twenty or twenty-five feet to where his coat was and got his pistol. Hermes was striking at him and the defendant fired four shots and killed him. The judge instructed the jury among other things that "it is necessary to remember, in considering the question of self-defense, that the party assaulted is always under the obligation to retreat, so long as retreat is open to him, provided he can do so without subjecting himself to the danger of death or great bodily harm." The instruction was reinforced by the further intimation that unless "retreat would have appeared to a man of reasonable prudence, in the position of the defendant, as involving danger of death or serious bodily harm" the defendant was not entitled to stand his ground. An instruction to the effect that if the defendant had reasonable grounds of apprehension that he was in danger of losing his life or of suffering serious bodily harm from Hermes he was not bound to retreat was refused. So the question is brought out with sufficient clearness whether the formula laid down by the Court and often repeated by the ancient law is adequate to the protection of the defendant's rights.

It is useless to go into the developments of the law from the time when a man who had killed another no matter how innocently had to get his ardon, whethe of grace or of course. Concrete cases or illustrations stated in the early law in conditions very different from the present, like the reference to retreat in Coke, Third Inst. 55, and elsewhere, have had a tendency to ossify into specific rules without much regard for reason. Other examples may be found in the law as to trespass *ab initio, Commonwealth* v. *Rubin,* 165 Massachusetts, 453, and as to fresh complaint after rape. *Commonwealth* v. *Cleary,* 172 Massachusetts, 175. Rationally the failure to retreat is a circumstance to be considered with all the others in order to determine whether the defendant went farther than he was justified in doing; not a categorical proof of guilt. The law has grown, and even if historical mistakes have contributed to its growth it has tended in the direction of rules consistent with human nature. Many respectable writers agree that if a man reasonably believes that he is in immediate danger of death or grievous bodily harm from his assailant he may stand his ground and that if he kills him he has not exceeded the bounds of lawful self-defense. That has been the decision of this Court.

Beard v. *United States,* 158 U.S. 550, 559. Detached reflection cannot be demanded in the presence of an uplifted knife. Therefore in this Court, at least, it is not a condition of immunity tht one in that situation should pause to consider whether a reasonable man might not think it possible to fly with safety or to disable his assailant rather than to kill him. *Rowe* v. *United States,* 164 U.S. 546, 558. The law of Texas very strongly adopts these views as is shown by many cases, of which it is enough to cite two. *Cooper* v. *State,* 49 Tex. Crim. Rep. 28, 38. *Baltrip* v. *State,* 30 Tex. Ct. App. 545, 549.

It is true that in the case of Beard he was upon his own land (not in his house), and in that of Rowe he was in the room of a hotel, but those facts, although mentioned by the Court, would not have bettered the defence by the old common law and were not appreciably more favorable than that the defendant here was at a place where he was called to be, in the discharge of his duty. There was evidence that the last shot was fired after Hermes was down. The jury might not believe the defendant's testimony that it was an accidental discharge, but the suggestion of the Government that this Court may disregard the considerable body of evidence that the shooting was in self-defense is based upon a misunderstanding of what was meant by some language in *Battle* v. *United States,* 209 U.S. 36, 38. Moreover if the last shot was intentional and may seem to have been unnecessary when considered in cold blood, the defendant would not necessarily lose his immunity if it followed close upon the others while the heat of the conflict was on, and if the defendant believed that he was fighting for his life.

The Government presents a different case. It denies that Hermes had a knife and even that Brown was acting in self-defence. Notwithstanding the repeated threats of Hermes and intimations that one of the two would die at the next encounter, which seem hardly to be denied, of course it was possible for the jury to find that Brown had not sufficient reason to think that his life was in danger at that time, that he exceeded the limits of reasonable self-defence or even tht he was the attacking party. But upon the hypothesis to which the evidence gave much color, that Hermes began the attack, the instruction that we have stated was wrong.

Judgment reversed.

MR. JUSTICE PITNEY and MR. JUSTICE CLARKE dissent.

Appendix F
SELF-DEFENSE PLEA AT NÜRNBERG

*Judgment of the Nürnberg
Tribunal, September 30, 1946*

* * *

On the 1st March, Hitler issued a directive regarding the Weser Exercise which contained the words:

"The development of the situation in Scandinavia requires the making of all preparations for the occupation of Denmark and Norway by a part of the German Armed Forces. This operation should prevent British encroachment on Scandinavia and the Baltic; further, it should guarantee our ore base in Sweden and give our Navy and Air Force a wider start line against Britain . . . The crossing of the Danish border and the landings in Norway must take place simultaneously. . . It is most important that the Scandinavian States as well as the Western opponents should be taken by surprise by our measures."

On the 24th March the naval operation orders for the Weser Exercise were issued, and on the 30th March the defendant Doenitz as Commander in Chief of U-boats issued his operational order for the occupation of Denmark and Norway. On the 9th April 1940, the German forces invaded Norway and Denmark.

. . .it is clear that as early as October 1939 the question of invading Norway was under consideration. The defense that has been made here is that Germany was compelled to attack Norway to forestall an Allied invasion, and her action was therefore preventive.

It must be remembered that preventive action in foreign territory is justified only in case of "an instant and overwhelming necessity for self-defense, leaving no choice of means and no moment of deliberation." (The Caroline Case, Moore's Digest of International Law, Vol. II, p. 412.) How widely the view was held in influential German circles that the Allies intended to occupy Norway cannot be determined with exactitude. Quisling asserted that the Allies would intervene in Norway with the tacit consent of the Norwegian Government. The German Legation at Oslo disagreed with this view, although the Naval Attaché at that Legation shared it.

* * *

...it is clear that when the plans for an attack on Norway were being made they were not made for the purpose of forestalling an imminent Allied landing, but, at the most, that they might prevent an Allied occupation at some future date.

When the final orders for the German invasion of Norway were given, the diary of the Naval Operations Staff for March 23, 1940, records:

"A mass encroachment by the English into Norwegian territorial waters... is not to be expected at the present time." And Admiral Assmann's entry for March 26 says:

"British landing in Norway not considered serious."

* * *

It was further argued that Germany alone could decide, in accordance with the reservations made by many of the Signatory Powers at the time of the conclusion of the Kellogg-Briand Pact, whether preventive action was a necessity, and that in making her decision her judgment was conclusive. But whether action taken under the claim of self-defense was in fact aggressive or defensive must ultimately be subject to investigation and adjudication if international law is ever to be enforced.

* * *

In the light of all the available evidence it is impossible to accept the contention that the invasions of Denmark and Norway were defensive, and in the opinion of the Tribunal they were acts of aggressive war.

INDEX

Abused spouse defense, 29
Aggressive rights, 13

Battered wife syndrome, 29-34
Brown v. United States, 2
Burden of proof, 31

"Castle" retreat rule, 19-21
Common law, 2

Deadly force, 7,9,23,32
Dicey's *Law of Constitution,* 52

Excusable self-defense, 1,3,24

Force, 27

Goetz, Bernard, 35-39
Grainger v. State, 26

Holmes, Justice, 25
Human rights, 51-52

Instructions, jury, 32

Justifiable self-defense, 1,7,8

Minority retreat rule, 21-22
Model Penal Code references, 15,17,24,26,27,33
Monroe Doctrine, 42

Non-deadly weapon aggressor, 13,23

People v. Lenkovich, 17
People v. Tomlins, 18

Retreat, 17
Rowe v. United States, 13

Shorter v. People, 25
State v. Broadhurst, 13
State v. Wanrow, 29

Teale v. State, 26

United Nations Charter, 44-46

Values, 49-54 passim
Vigil v. People, 26

Withdrawal, 14